The Auditor's
Report and
Investor Behavior

The Auditor's Report and Investor Behavior

WITHDRAWN

Ralph Estes
Wichita State University

LexingtonBooks
D.C. Heath and Company
Lexington, Massachusetts
Toronto

Library of Congress Cataloging in Publication Data

Estes, Ralph W.
 The auditor's report and investor behavior.

 Includes bibliographical references and index.
 1. Auditors' reports. 2. Investments. I. Title.
HF5667.6.E83   657'.452   82-47774
ISBN 0-669-05584-0   AACR2

Copyright © 1982 by D.C. Heath and Company

Published simultaneously in Canada

Printed in the United States of America

International Standard Book Number: 0-669-05584-0

Library of Congress Catalog Card Number: 82-47774

Contents

List of Figures
and Tables

Preface

In our complex society the accountant's certificate and the lawyer's opinion can be instruments for inflicting pecuniary loss more potent than the chisel or the crowbar.

—*U.S.* v. *Benjamin* (1964)

Consider the audit report on financial statements. It is mandated largely by one group, defined and controlled by another, paid for by a third, and directed toward a fourth. It is required by the Securities and Exchange Commission, controlled by the American Institute of Certified Public Accountants, paid for by audited companies, and directed toward an amorphous group of presumed users of financial statements, primarily consisting of investors and lenders. What is the likelihood that such a process will produce a product that is worth more than it costs?

This is a perfectly valid question—indeed, one that should be asked—but we are in no position to answer it. We could develop a pretty good estimate of the audit reports' aggregate costs, but to estimate its value we must first determine its effects. Since audit reports are addressed to human readers, this means that we must attempt to separate, from all the stimuli that affect human behavior, the effects that can be traced with some degree of confidence to the audit report and to the audit report only.

This study is a step—and I hope a significant step—in that direction. It represents a major effort to identify and measure, through a series of controlled experiments, the differential effects of the standard audit report as well as the effects of the *except for, subject to,* adverse, and disclaimer versions of that report. Seven measures are used to encapsulate investor behavior.

Investor behavior cannot, of course, be captured in seven variables, nor can an experiment tell us conclusively how investors will behave in an actual investment setting. But because of this study's broad scope, the statistical controls employed, the large samples obtained, and the realism of the experimental tasks, the results should be considerably more reliable than those obtained from simplistic experiments or surveys, and should therefore provide a quantum addition to our knowledge of the effects of audit reports on investor behavior.

This book is based on the final stages of research that proceeded through several stages over the course of seven years. Support provided by the Wichita State University General Research Fund is gratefully acknowledged, and special thanks are due to Research Assistants Jan Kennedy and Mike Hein.

Introduction

Audits have become a pervasive part of our lives. We face financial-statement audits, tax audits, energy audits, social audits, cash audits, performance audits, management audits, and compliance audits. As government, business, and society grow in complexity, the desire for assurance also grows—assurance that things are as they appear to be or are reported to be.

Audits are expensive. A senior partner in an accounting firm will charge over $100 an hour. An audit of a small business will cost thousands of dollars, while audit fees for larger organizations can easily run into six figures, with fees in the millions of dollars frequently encountered. Collectively audits account for probably $2 to $4 billion annually in the U.S. economy.

The audit function initially developed as a means of checking on reports made by agents to their principals; for example, the Bible tells of kings appointing auditors to check on the collections made by tax agents in occupied lands. The greatest impetus was provided by colonial capitalists who sought verification of the reports sent back by agents in distant colonies.

Prior to the twentieth century, reports on a company or branch were desired by only a small number of owners, investors, or creditors. These financiers could and did engage auditors on their own behalf. Reports rarely went to outside parties and there was little need to provide an auditor's assurance to the general public.

The twentieth century growth in share ownership brought a need for some means of assuring that shareowners and potential investors would be provided with reliable financial information. Congress reacted to this need with the Securities Acts of 1933 and 1934, which require an independent auditor's opinion on financial statements as a condition for listing a corporation's shares on a securities exchange. Thus the demand for independent audits is now derived primarily from a legal requirement, and no longer directly from interested parties. Audits may be required by banks in evaluating loan applications, by potential merger partners, and by other parties with a direct interest, but audits of companies listed on securities exchanges account for the largest fees and the greatest influence on audit procedures and reporting standards.

The demand for audit services is not determined by a free market (Commission on Auditors' Responsibilities 1978, p. 51). The demand is an

1

indirect or derived demand imposed by securities laws passed nearly a half-century ago. In the absence of market evidence of demand, it becomes appropriate to consider critically whether the auditor's report on financial statements provides utility and, if so, to whom and in what respect. Are commensurate benefits received in return for the billions paid each year for financial-statement audits?

Unfortunately these questions cannot be addressed until much more is known about the effects of audit reports. For example, does a given form of audit opinion have, on the average, a positive effect, a negative effect, or no effect on investor attitudes and behavior with respect to the audited company and its securities. Many have been willing to offer a priori, presumptive answers to this question, but research evidence is virtually nonexistent.

This book describes and presents the results of a research study designed to increase our knowledge of the effects of financial-statement audit reports on investor behavior. The need for this kind of research has been expressed by a number of commentators, including the American Accounting Association's Committee on Basic Auditing Concepts (1973, p. 52):

> In most cases today, the intended effect of the auditor's report is not clear and the effects it does produce are not well known. More consideration needs to be given to this area and greater research needs to be performed. Communication is not neutral. It does have an impact and can change behavior. Failure to consider this important aspect may be detrimental to the purpose of the audit and jeopardize the entire contribution of the audit process.

A call by top accounting officials of the U.S. Securities and Exchange Commission (SEC) for research into the behavior of those receiving audit reports provided much of the direct impetus for this study:

> At the present time, very little is known about how people react to auditors' reports. For example, we do not know the response to the unqualified opinion, qualified opinion, or disclaimer of opinion wordings that appear in a standard auditor's "certificate." (Burton and Sampson 1976, p. 223)

Research on the differential effects of the several report forms was also called for by Knoll (1976). The present study addresses the behavioral effects of the unqualified opinion, two qualified-opinion forms, the adverse opinion, and the disclaimer of opinion.

Given the number of people in the auditing arm of the accounting profession, the bureaucracies in both the public and the private sectors that have evolved to regulate it, the monetary costs of audits, and the delays and disruptions they cause for reporting companies, it is surprising that the audit and its end product, the audit report, have not been subjected to thorough and critical research. Fortunately, there does appear to be a quickening of interest among researchers in these important areas (see chapter 2 for a review).

What are the results of a financial-statement audit? There are undoubtedly effects on the audited organization and its personnel, but the most obvious and tangible result is a brief report expressing the certified public accountant's (CPA's) opinion on the fairness of the financial statements. This report is variously and synonymously called an accountant's, auditor's, or audit report, opinion, or certificate.

If all is in order the report will be in the following, highly standardized form prescribed by the American Institute of Certified Public Accountant's (AICPA) Statement on Auditing Standards Number 15 (AICPA 1976):

> We have examined the balance sheets of ABC Company as of December 31, 19X2 and 19X1, and the related statements of income, retained earnings, and changes in financial position for the years then ended. Our examinations were made in accordance with generally accepted auditing standards and, accordingly, included such tests of the accounting records and such other auditing procedures as we considered necessary in the circumstances.
>
> In our opinion, the financial statements referred to above present fairly the financial position of ABC Company as of December 31, 19X2 and 19X1, and the results of its operations and the changes in its financial position for the years then ended, in conformity with generally accepted accounting principles applied on a consistent basis.

The first standard wording was adopted in 1923. The present form was essentially adopted in 1939, although minor changes have been made from time to time. The most recent change, for example, added the phrase "and the changes in its financial position."

If the financial statements are not consistent from one year to the next in the application of accounting principles, and the auditor agrees with the change, the last part of the second paragraph is reworded as follows (AICPA 1972):

> . . . applied on a consistent basis after restatement for the change, with which we concur, in the method of accounting for _____ as described in Note _____ to the financial statements.

This is referred to as a consistency exception. Effects of consistency exceptions have been investigated in a number of studies, and were, therefore, omitted from the scope of the present study to reduce the burden on the experimental subjects.

When financial statements are not presented fairly in accordance with generally accepted accounting principles, generally accepted auditing standards require the auditor to explain the departure in a middle paragraph of the audit report and take exception along the following lines in the opinion paragraph (AICPA 1974):

> In our opinion, except for the effects of _____ as discussed in the preceding paragraph, the financial statements present fairly . . .

To the auditor, this is an unfavorable comment of some significance. It is generally assumed among accountants that an *except for* opinion has detrimental effects, perhaps influencing the evaluations of the company by security analysts and counselors and depressing the market for the company's securities. Auditors are consequently reluctant to issue an *except for* opinion, and go to considerable lengths to persuade the reporting company's management to revise the statements to bring them into line with generally accepted accounting principles. In the majority of cases, it appears, management does make the necessary changes, evidently because it shares the auditor's view of the probable negative effects of an *except for* opinion. There is an even more potent factor for companies whose securities are listed: the Securities and Exchange Commission will generally refuse to accept, for filing, statements accompanied by an *except for* qualified opinion (or an adverse opinion).

Substantial uncertainty with respect to the effects of future events may give rise to an opinion qualification. The matter is explained in a middle paragraph, and language similar to the following is added to the opinion paragraph (AICPA 1974):

> In our opinion, subject to the effects, if any, on the financial statements of the ultimate resolution of the matter discussed in the preceding paragraph, the financial statements referred to above present fairly . . .

Unlike the *except for* qualification, the *subject to* opinion is not viewed by auditors as negative in the sense of reflecting a disagreement over the presentation of the financial statements; the uncertainty may require a qualification, but it may be nobody's fault.

In rare instances the auditor will conclude that the financial statements taken as a whole are not fairly presented. In such cases a paragraph or paragraphs are added to explain all the substantive reasons for the adverse opinion, and the opinion paragraph follows wording similar to the following (AICPA 1974):

> In our opinion, because of the effects of the matters discussed in the preceding paragraph, the financial statements referred to above do not present fairly, in conformity with generally accepted accounting principles, the financial position of X Company as of December 31, 19XX, or the results of its operations and changes in its financial position for the year then ended.

Auditors view this as the most extreme, and most negative, of the several opinion variations. It is issued only rarely.

A disclaimer of opinion is issued when the auditor has not performed an examination sufficient in scope or when sufficient evidence cannot be obtained to permit the formation of an opinion on the financial statements as a whole, or when such material uncertainty exists concerning the outcome and effects of future events that an overall opinion cannot be formed. The reason for the disclaimer is stated in a middle paragraph, and the opinion paragraph is worded along the following lines (AICPA 1974):

> Because of the uncertainty associated with the matter referred to in the preceding paragraph, we are not able to express, and do not express, an opinion on the financial statements referred to above.

There is concern in the professional accounting community that a disclaimer is interpreted as providing some form of assurance concerning the financial statements, instead of being no opinion at all. Apparently the presence of any report from a CPA, without regard to the wording, is reassuring to some.

Other departures from the standard report are possible, but the most important ones, in terms of potential impact on investor behavior, have been discussed.

When comparative financial statements are presented, the audit reports are carefully worded to indicate the particular kind of opinion that is rendered on each year's statements. It would be possible to have any combination of opinions (standard and adverse, disclaimer and *except for, subject to* and standard, and so forth) covering the two years.

The AICPA annually tabulates the audit reports issued for 600 large companies. In 1979 audit reports on statements of thirty companies were qualified because of uncertainty, and reports on ninety-seven companies received consistency qualifications (AICPA 1980). One disclaimer is cited, but no adverse opinions or *except for* qualifications were tabulated.

CPAs spend a great deal of time and demonstrate a tremendous amount of concern (within their firms, if not necessarily publicly) over the exact and proper wording of audit reports. Clearly they believe that audit reports and their form and precise wording make a difference.

The study reported in this book is an effort to test just that question—do audit reports have any effect, and do their separate forms make any difference, as far as investors are concerned?

This book proceeds to a review of prior research on the auditor's report in chapter 2, development of a theoretical perspective in chapter 3, explanation of the experimental research design and analysis in chapter 4, and presentation of results in chapter 5. The book concludes, in chapter 6, with a summarization and consideration of implications.

Prior Research on the Auditor's Report

Formal, systematic research in accounting is a relatively recent phenomenon; for practical purposes 1960 can be used as a convenient point to mark its beginning in any volume. Earlier research in the 1960s was concerned largely with financial accounting. Some argued that auditing research was not "academically respectable" during those earlier years, but, whether this was true or not, little auditing research was undertaken during the 1960s.

This picture changed in the 1970s. Stimulated perhaps by the need to continuously find new areas for research to meet their universities' expectations and by the Peat, Marwick, Mitchell and Co. Research Opportunities in Auditing program (1976), accounting professors began to seriously investigate auditing issues. They were joined in these efforts by a small number of accounting practitioners. (Of the forty-two studies discussed in this chapter, thirty-eight were published after 1970.)

There is a growing body of scientific knowledge about auditors and their work. The research has sometimes been shoddy and the results contradictory, but this seems reasonable for a widely diffused effort with no central direction that is less than twenty years old. Research must always be viewed critically, but when placed in perspective—lack of general agreement on problems and goals; limited funds and more limited rewards; disorder and inconclusive evidence in the "mother" disciplines of psychology, sociology, and economics; and a very late start up the learning curve—the accumulation of research in auditing is reasonably impressive.

In this chapter, prior research on the auditor's report is reviewed in terms of whether the report is read, how well it is understood, and its effects on behavior and attitudes. Because the sources are so dispersed and some may, therefore, be inaccessible to the reader, an effort has been made to provide a comprehensive survey.

Readership

A number of researchers have been interested in the extent to which the auditor's report is read. They have used either interviews or mail surveys to obtain data from stockholders, financial analysts, bankers, and others.

Arthur Andersen & Co. (1974). A study commissioned by the accounting firm of Arthur Andersen & Co. (see bibliography) and performed by Opinion Research Corporation included a question about readership. The 404 shareowners interviewed reported that they read the auditor's report:

All of the time	19%
Most of the time	31
Only sometimes	28
Rarely or never	21
No response	1

Barnett (1976). For a doctoral dissertation at Texas Tech University, Barnett surveyed Texas investors to assess their understanding of the auditor's report. Both professional investors (110 responding) and nonprofessional investors (277 responses) ranked annual reports as the prime source of relevant information about companies, with stockbrokers ranked as the second most important source. The two groups gave the following responses concerning their readership of the audit report:

	Professionals	*Nonprofessionals*
Companies whose stock is already owned		
Always read	34.9%	43.8%
Usually read	30.3	27.2
Sometimes read	22.0	14.8
Rarely read	11.9	11.8
Never read	0.9	2.4
Companies being considered for investment		
Always read	34.9%	38.0%
Usually read	24.5	29.7
Sometimes read	24.5	13.3
Rarely read	14.2	15.8
Never read	1.9	3.2

Contrary to most expectations and to results obtained in other studies, Barnett's research indicates that nonprofessional investors are somewhat more likely to read the auditor's report than are professionals.

Brenner (1971). Brenner surveyed investors and bank loan-officers obtaining 1,241 responses. The questionnaire asked about readership of several items in the annual report, with the following results for the auditor's opinion (results have been adjusted to eliminate "no answer" responses):

	Bankers	Analysts	Stockholders
Read very carefully	44%	33%	15%
Read somewhat carefully	28	30	27
Did not read carefully	21	26	30
Did not read	7	11	28

Brenner's study indicates that, of the three groups surveyed, bankers read the auditor's report most carefully and stockholders read it the least.

Clift (1973). Of thirty-six professional investors interviewed in Australia, 28 percent indicated they are interested in the auditor's report only if it is qualified, while 19 percent labeled the report "not very important." These results are difficult to compare with those obtained in other studies because of the small sample size as well as the overlapping and noncomparable response categories.

Epstein (1975). Epstein surveyed shareholders nationwide, obtaining 432 responses. They were asked to rank, in terms of usefulness, seven items in the annual report—income statement, statement of financial position, statement of changes in financial position, footnotes, auditor's report, president's letter, essay and pictorial material. Shareholders indicated that the auditor's report is least useful and is read least thoroughly of these items. One-third of the respondents said they do not even read the auditor's report, and 56 percent said it is not useful.

Fess and Ziegler (1977). In a study for the Commission on Auditors' Responsibilities (an independent commission established by the AICPA) Fess and Ziegler surveyed financial analysts (118 responses), bankers (214 responses), and individual shareholders (188 responses). The respondents were asked two questions concerning readership of the auditor's report, with the following results:

	Financial Analysts	Bankers	Individual Shareholders
"How often do you look for the auditor's report when examining the annual report of corporations?"			
Always	55.1%	87.4%	40.4%
Often	23.7	7.5	22.9
Sometimes	16.1	3.7	21.8
Almost never	5.1	1.4	14.9

	Financial Analysts	Bankers	Individual Shareholders
"How carefully do you read the auditor's report?"			
Carefully	28.0%	69.2%	27.3%
Hurriedly	70.3	30.8	56.9
Note that it is there	1.7	0.0	15.8

The dominant reason given by all three groups for not reading the auditor's report carefully is that they are "already familiar with it," although nearly one-third of the responding shareholders indicated that they do not read the report because they are "interested only that it's there." Many shareholders thus appear to be interested in whether an audit has been performed, but not in the specific wording of the auditor's opinion.

Georgeson and Company/Graham-Chisholm Company (1972). Personnel of these two companies interviewed 219 small stockholders and seventy-three security analysts regarding their annual-report readership. The stockholders were asked the open-ended question, "What sections of the annual report were you most interested in, least interested in?" The auditor's report was cited by less than 1 percent in response to each question. (Even photos did better, being listed by 2 percent as the section "most interested in.")

Security analysts were only slightly more interested in the auditor's report. They were asked, "Which sections do you read first and which do you find least interesting?" The auditor's report was listed as "read first" by 2 percent and as least interesting by 1 percent.

These results, although somewhat confusing, seem to suggest that stockholders and security analysts are not particularly interested in the auditor's report but are not inclined to list it as unimportant.

Lee and Tweedie (1975a). A United Kingdom survey of stockholders of a London-based engineering company, with 374 replies, found that the auditor's report is the least read of seven annual report items (chairman's report, profit and loss account, directors' report, balance sheet, notes to accounts, statistical data, and auditor's report). Actual responses for the auditor's report were

Read thoroughly	17.4%
Read briefly for interest	39.0
Not read at all	43.6

The auditor's report was also given the lowest importance rating among the seven items.

Lee and Tweedie (1977). In a subsequent, more intensive United Kingdom study 301 shareholders interviewed provided almost identical answers concerning the extent of audit-report readership:

Read thoroughly	16%
Read briefly for interest	36
Not read at all	48

Given the range of results obtained in other studies, it is reassuring to note that two studies in the same country using the same categories produced very similar results, although data were collected by mail survey in the first and through interviews in the second.

Stobie (1978). Stobie surveyed financial-statement users in South Africa, obtaining responses from ninety-one investment analysts, seventy-six corporate managers ("directors"), sixty individual shareholders, and forty-six others. Over twenty questions were asked, including the following: "Do you always read the audit report when examining a set of financial statements?" Roughly two-thirds of the respondents answered in the affirmative:

Investment analysts	63%
Corporate managers	72
Individual shareholders	65

The several studies just reviewed generally used different classifications and were undertaken in different areas or countries. Comparisons are thus difficult, but it is evident that the auditor's report is not read by a substantial number of those for whom it is intended. Stockholders appear to be less likely to read the auditor's report than investment analysts and bankers.

The auditor's report communicates a message—or several messages. Communication may occur when a person merely observes that an audit report is appended to financial statements, without actually reading it. The report may serve as a signal that an audit has been performed, and may be interpreted to mean that the auditor has ensured that the financial statements have been properly presented. In this case the report may not actually be read, but may, nevertheless, have informational content (although not always the information the auditor intended to communicate) and may influence behavior.

Financial-statement users may also observe the number of paragraphs and general length of the auditor's report without reading further. Two short paragraphs mean a standard or clean opinion that need not be read, while three paragraphs serve as a signal for something out of the ordinary. Since most financial statements receive the standard, two-paragraph opinion, we might expect that many people would indicate that they do not read the audit report. Despite all the research conducted on audit-report readership, this leaves us rather uncertain as to the significance and impact of the communication effort reflected in the auditor's report. Fortunately, other studies have investigated the understanding of the auditor's opinion and its impact on behavior, attitudes, and decisions.

Understanding

Communication models require, among other elements, a sender, a message, and a receiver. The message must be received before communication can occur, and, for a written report, this means it must be read or at least perceived. The message must also be understood; reasonable congruence is required between the message intended by the sender and its interpretation by the receiver. This aspect of the audit-reporting process has also been addressed in a number of studies.

Arthur Andersen & Co. (1974). A substantial minority of shareowners, 37 percent, erroneously think an accounting firm determines the accuracy of financial statements by going through all financial records. Even greater misunderstanding was revealed concerning the auditor's responsibility for detection of fraud. Interviewees were asked whether they agreed or disagreed that "the most important function of the public accounting firm's audit of a corporation is to detect significant fraud," with the following results:

	Percentage Agreeing
Business press	68%
Shareowners	66
Analysts/brokers	55
Institutional investors	39
Corporate executives	20
Securities lawyers	18
Government officials	16
Business professors (primarily in accounting)	12
Certified public accountants	6

These results are especially significant because they indicate that the intended external beneficiaries of a financial-statement audit misunderstand its purpose more than do members of other groups.

Ashworth (1963). In an early study, Ashworth interviewed CPAs and bankers. Less than half the CPAs thought that their clients' bankers clearly understood the meanings of an unqualified and a qualified opinion, and a disclaimer. According to Ashworth, this view was supported by the interviews with bankers; a few bankers even thought that, in signing a qualified opinion, a CPA is admitting a poor standard of work.

Beck (1973). Questionnaires were returned by 711 Australian shareholders in this study. They reflected significant misunderstanding of the auditor's role. There was substantial agreement (over 90 percent) that the work of the auditor should give assurance that the financial statements are reliable and that the accounting system is effective and has been operating efficiently. But a substantial majority of the shareholders also expect the auditor's work to give assurance that no frauds have been perpetrated by company officials (93 percent), management has discharged all statutory duties (92 percent), management is efficient (71 percent), and the company is financially sound (81 percent).

Bennett (1976). For a University of South Carolina dissertation, Bennett adapted the semantic differential to study the meaning to stockholders, public accountants, and management accountants, of the phrases *fairly presents, generally accepted accounting principles,* and *consistently applied* in the auditor's opinion. Bennett concluded that the semantic meanings of the three phrases were significantly different among all three groups.

Briloff (1966). Briloff surveyed sixty-four accountants and seventy-two members of the financial community. He found that the two groups were not in agreement on the meaning of *present fairly . . . in conformity with generally accepted accounting principles,* nor could they agree on the form of opinion that would be issued when management has selected a particular, acceptable accounting principle but the auditor prefers another.

Corless and Norgaard (1974). This study was concerned with user reactions to a forecasted statement of operations. Responses to a mail survey were received from 264 financial analysts (all in either Boston, Massachusetts; New York City; or Hartford, Connecticut); responses were also obtained from eighty MBA students at the University of Connecticut. Respondents correctly understood that, in a report accompanying the forecast, the CPA had not attested to the accuracy of the forecast (5.3 percent thought he had, 89.2 percent thought he had not, and 5.6 percent could not tell).

Epstein (1975). In this survey of shareholders, 22 percent indicated they have difficulty understanding the auditor's report. Of seven items in the annual report, the auditor's report was ranked fourth in difficulty of understanding, more difficult than the income statement, but less difficult than the other financial statements.

Fess and Ziegler (1977). In a mail survey, respondents were asked directly, "How well do you believe you understand the auditor's report?" with the following results:

	Financial Analysts (n = 118)	Bankers (n = 214)	Individual Shareholders (n = 188)
Completely	41.9%	49.3%	33.3%
Most of it	53.0	49.3	52.0
Much of it	4.3	1.4	12.6
Do not understand it	0.8	0.0	2.1

Whether or not financial-statement users are confused over the meaning of the auditor's report as indicated in some other studies, according to these data, they *think* they understand it. Any communication problem would be heightened by such overconfidence.

Lee (1970). Auditors, auditees, and "audit beneficiaries" were surveyed in the United Kingdom (the number responding was not reported) and asked to identify current audit objectives. Their answers indicated significant misunderstandings, even among auditors. While the primary objective (to give an opinion on the truth and fairness of the financial accounts of the company in relation to company legislation and generally accepted accounting principles) was identified by more than 90 percent of the respondents in each group, substantial numbers also cited preventing major fraud and error in the company (over 80 percent of the *auditors* identified this as a current objective), insuring that all legal requirements have been complied with by the company, guaranteeing the accuracy of the financial accounts, and examining and giving an opinion on the efficiency and adequacy of the company's management and its operations.

Lee and Tweedie (1975b). In a survey of United Kingdom shareholders approximately 10 percent supported the erroneous view that the legal responsibility for a company's annual financial report is in the hands of the company's auditors.

Lee and Tweedie (1977). Based on interviews with 301 United Kingdom shareholders, the authors concluded that shareholders' understanding of the auditor's report could be classified as follows:

Reasonable	41%
Vague	20
None	39

While these results do suggest a poor level of understanding, scale-weighted responses indicate that only the chairman's report is better understood, while the director's report, profit and loss account, and balance sheet are less understood than the auditor's report. This may place the auditor's report in perspective, but does not instill confidence in its communicative effectiveness.

Libby (1979a). An experiment was conducted using thirty Chicago audit firm partners and twenty-eight commercial-loan officers from five large Chicago banks. Subjects were presented with pairs of audit reports, each labeled as to type (such as disclaimer, uncertainty, litigation). The study was limited to variations of scope limitation and uncertainty reports. Subjects compared each pair of reports and indicated similarity on a ten-point scale, and also scaled each report on thirteen adjective pairs. Differences between the auditors and bankers were not significant, and Libby concludes: "This general finding of no large differences implies that fears of miscommunication of the messages intended by audit reports to more sophisticated users may not be justified."

Oliver (1974). The semantic differential was used to test communication between CPAs and others interested in financial reporting. The concepts tested were accounting, income determination, consistency, disclosure, matching, value(ation), cost, revenues, and expenses; of these, only consistency specifically appears in the auditor's report. Oliver concluded that a communication base exists between most groups interested in financial reporting and that "the CPAs generally possess concept meanings similar to the members of the five professional user groups."

Purdy, Smith, and Gray (1969). A real, but disguised, annual report was used in an experimental context, with footnotes and the auditor's report varied with respect to placement and the inclusion or exclusion of a statement concerning deviance from an Accounting Principles Board opinion on leases. The experiment was administered to eighty-two members of the Institute of Internal Auditors, thirty-four members of the Financial Executives Institute, forty-two executives with a fire-insurance company, and twenty-five executives in a commercial bank. They found that the method of disclosure of the deviation—in the auditor's report or in the financial-statement footnotes—makes no difference in whether the information is retained by the reader. They also concluded that the deviation was perceived and retained better when an auditor's report containing a paragraph describing the deviation and its effects is placed after, rather than before, the financial statements.

Shank, Dillard, and Murdock (1978 and 1979); Dillard, Murdock, and Shank (1978); Shank, Dillard, and Bylinski (1979). In these studies the same approach was used with each of the following groups:

	Number Responding
Bank loan officers	304
Financial analysts	207
Corporate financial officers	307
Partners in large CPA firms	232

A questionnaire was mailed that presented eight contingency situations taken from actual annual reports, and that provided five options for disclosure of the contingency. From the lowest to the highest level of disclosure, these were (1) no reference, (2) disclosure in unaudited section of annual report, (3) footnote disclosure, (4) footnote disclosure plus a three-paragraph *subject to* audit opinion, and (5) disclaimer. The respondents were asked, among other things, to indicate how the several contingencies should be disclosed. A comparison of their responses with the manner of disclosure actually used in the annual report provides an indication of the level of understanding of the audit process and the auditor's report:

	Bank loan officers	*Financial analysts*	*Corporate financial officers*	*CPA firm partners*
Respondent preferred a higher level of disclosure	46.2%	40.1%	31.5%	30.0%
Respondent's choice agreed with actual disclosure level	39.3	44.2	48.1	52.7
Respondent preferred a lower level of disclosure	14.4	15.7	20.4	17.3

Interpretation of these results must depend upon one's prior expectations, but they can hardly be taken to indicate widespread agreement between auditors and their principal, or at least their more sophisticated, audiences. For that matter there is a disturbing lack of agreement among CPAs concerning the appropriate level of disclosure and form of opinion to be rendered in a particular situation. These data suggest that a substantial number of financial-statement users and even CPAs would prefer a higher level of disclosure, that is, greater use of *subject to* opinions and disclaimers, than that actually found in practice.

Stobie (1978). Stobie surveyed the following groups (with number of responses indicated):

Shareholders	55
Company directors	76
Investment analysts	91

The responses often reflected substantial misunderstanding of the nature and purpose of an audit and the auditor's report. Nearly one-third of the shareholders and one-fourth of company directors believe that auditors examine all financial records in conducting an audit. Significant numbers (27 percent of shareholders, 33 percent of company directors, and 16 percent of investment analysts) indicated that the auditor's report "guarantees the accuracy and amounts" in audited financial statements. Roughly one-third of respondents in each group expect the unqualified audit report to provide assurance that the company's accounting system is effective. Finally, many respondents expect the unqualified audit report to provide assurance that management is efficient, the company is sound financially, and no frauds have occurred. Of the three groups, investment analysts indicated the best understanding of the audit and audit report (although from 10 to 20 percent of the analysts reflected distorted impressions) and shareholders the worst.

These studies, conducted at different times in different countries by different researchers using different methods, naturally did not produce uniform results. Nevertheless, a reasonably clear picture emerges.

The general view that bankers and security analysts understand the auditor's role and report better than do shareholders is confirmed. Most financial-statement users understand the primary role of a financial-statement audit, but large numbers, especially among shareholders, believe the audit is intended to prevent fraud and to provide assurance against it, as well as to provide assurance that management is efficient and that the company is sound. Agreement is poor between auditors and their audiences on the meaning of phrases in the standard opinion, and on the form of opinion that should be rendered when significant uncertainty exists.

Interviews and questionnaire surveys indicate a poor understanding of the auditor's report, but self-assessment by shareholders and others suggest that financial-statement users are not fully aware of their state of confusion. In the communication model the receiver must understand the message as intended by the sender for full communication to occur; when communication does not occur, but the receiver believes it has, the receiver's resulting behavior should be largely unresponsive to the sender's (auditor's) intended message. This possibility has been investigated in studies on the effects of audit reports.

Effects

Research into the effects of audit reports on financial-statement users has intensified in the last few years. This has been especially true of market-based and experimental studies. A body of knowledge is accumulating that should provide insight into the impact of the auditor's work, and should also provide a foundation for investigation of the value of audits. This latter issue has been intractable in the absence of knowledge about the nature and direction of effect.

Market-based studies, often using the *market model*,[a] investigate the reaction of market prices to different forms of the audit opinion. They seek to determine the aggregate reaction to the auditor's report, but are necessarily limited, in the United States, to investigation of those forms of audit opinion tolerated by the SEC. Thus market-based studies are generally restricted to the standard opinion, an opinion qualified for uncertainty (the *subject to* opinion), and an opinion qualified for lack of consistency. Other opinion forms may be issued for companies whose securities are listed on an exchange, but these do not occur frequently.

Market-based studies cannot deal with the confounding effect of the information that forms the basis for an opinion qualification, on the one

---

[a]Market-based studies typically use the *market model* to assess the effect of an event, such as an earnings announcement or issuance of the annual report. The *market model* is a simple linear-regression model, usually of the following form:

$$R_{it} = \alpha_i + \beta_i R_{Mt} + \epsilon_{it}$$

where:

R_{it} = the rate of return of security i in period t, equal to $(P_{it} + D_{it}) / (P_{it-1})$, and

P_{it} = price of security i at the end of period t

P_{it-1} = price of security i at the end of period $t - 1$ (or the beginning of period t)

D_{it} = dividend paid by security i during period t

R_{Mt} = the rate of return on the market portfolio in period t, sometimes measured by Standard and Poor's Composite Index of 500 Stocks or the New York Stock Exchange Index.

The coefficient β_i measures a security's *systematic* risk, and indicates how the security's return behaves in relation to the average market return. The error term, ϵ_{it}, reflects the security's *unsystematic* risk, and embodies all the factors (other than overall market movements) that affect the individual security's return.

The *market model* may be used to investigate the impact of different audit-opinion forms or other factors on the residual term, ϵ_{it}, or on the risk of the security as measured by β_i. See Kaplan (1978) for a more complete discussion.

hand, and the form of the audit opinion on the other. In other words, the effect of opinion form alone, while controlling for the effect of the factor referred to in the qualification, cannot be effectively investigated in a study based on aggregate market data. Bailey (1982) has particularly challenged market-based studies on this point.

These problems can be overcome with an experimental approach. Control can be established over the separate effects of opinion form and the uncertainty or deviance on which the qualification is based, opinion forms can be varied at will, and individual reaction can be assessed. On the other hand, subjects may behave and respond differently in an experiment and in real-life decision settings.

The problems with market-based studies and experiments might suggest observation and measurement of individual behavior in a wide variety of actual decision settings, but the extreme cost of such an approach has prevented it from being used in research on the effect of the auditor's report.

Several researchers have simply asked financial-statement users directly about the effects of the auditor's report. This approach, while simple and inexpensive, relies on the willingness and ability of respondents to assess and describe their own behavior in hypothetical situations.

Market-Based Studies

Alderman (1977). In this study, twenty companies that had received at least one uncertainty qualification during the years 1968-1971 were matched with twenty firms that had received only unqualified audit opinions during those years. Analyzing price behavior over the three-year periods preceding and following the uncertainty qualification, Alderman concluded that "uncertainty qualifications had little impact on market-assessed risk," and the qualification therefore provided little information of value concerning risk to investors.

Alderman's study actually deals more with the effect of formal communication and emphasis of the uncertainty than with the effect of a qualified audit opinion. Because the possible effects of the uncertainty communication and the opinion form are always combined for a published annual report, this methodology cannot isolate any separate opinion-form effect. Given the volatility of market-price behavior, Alderman's study might also be questioned because of the small sample size.

Ball, Walker, and Whittred (1979). The market model was used to investigate the effects of 117 qualifications issued on 101 Australian firms over the period 1961-1972. The most common qualification was for a failure to record depreciation expense on buildings (a statement issued in 1970 by the Institute of Chartered Accountants in Australia effectively required firms to calculate depreciation on buildings, contrary to common previous practice). While most of the qualifications used the words *subject to,* these would have been *except for* qualifications in the United States; they relate mainly to noncompliance with appropriate accounting principles. This study is significant since accounting-principles qualifications are normally not accepted by the SEC, rarely appear in corporate annual reports in the United States, and thus cannot be investigated as to effect using market data.

Overall, the sample produced no significant effect on prices, but the set of qualifications for failure to record depreciation appear to have produced an upward revision in share prices. The authors have no plausible explanation for this result.

This study does not isolate the effect of opinion form from the effect of the exception information. No answer is provided to the question: Would the results have been the same if the exceptions had been communicated in footnotes and the auditors' opinions had been unqualified?

Baskin (1972). The market model was applied to a sample of 137 companies listed on the New York Stock Exchange, to study the effects of consistency exceptions in the auditor's report. (Since the standard audit opinion indicates that accounting principles have been consistently applied in the current and preceding year, any change in application of principles, such as a change in depreciation method, requires an exception in the auditor's report with regard to consistency.) Baskin concluded that "the consistency exception does not appear to have information content for most investors." Baskin's results have been questioned, however, on the grounds of misspecification of the measurement model (Alderman 1977, p. 23).

Firth (1978). The market model was used in this United Kingdom study to assess the effects of the 247 qualified audit reports issued for the 1,500 largest stock-exchange-listed firms for the years 1974 and 1975. A control group was created by pairing each company that received a qualified opinion with a company in the same industry and approximately the same size that received a clean opinion. Price movements in shares of the control and test groups were calculated for a period beginning twenty days prior to the release of the annual report and ending twenty days after its release. Since earnings and dividends announcements are made several weeks prior to the release of the annual report, this information should have been impounded in share prices prior to the study period. Three types of audit report qualification produced statistically significant (95 percent confidence level) price changes:

Type of qualification	Percentage difference between actual price and expected price as given by the market model
Statements do not present a "true and fair view" (similar to an adverse opinion in the Untied States, except that details for the qualification are usually not spelled out in the United Kingdom)	− 2.1
Going concern—if bankers withdrew their support, the firm would be forced into bankruptcy (similar to a *subject to* qualification or a disclaimer in the United States)	− 4.1
Asset valuation, due to auditor concern over possible overvaluation of fixed assets and receivables	− 5.0

The following qualifications produced only small price movements that were not statistically significant:

Accounts of a subsidiary not audited or audited by a different accounting firm.

Failure to comply with Statements of Standard Accounting Practice (SSAPs)—similar to an *except for* qualification in the United States for noncompliance with generally accepted accounting principles.

Failure to comply with SSAPs but the auditor concurs with the alternative accounting treatment used.

Continuing qualifications, where the company receives the same qualification year after year; these are presumably anticipated by the stock market and thus do not result in a significant price effect on the date of issuance.

The Firth study, like that by Ball, Walker, and Whittred, provides evidence concerning the effects of other than *subject to* type qualifications on investors.

Frishkoff and Rogowski (1978). This study is unique among market-based studies because it addresses the effect of the disclaimer form of audit report. A search of the AICPA's National Automated Accounting Research System (NAARS) file for the two-year period ending June 30, 1974, produced twenty-two disclaimers; sufficient price data were available from the *Wall Street Journal* on only ten of these, which were used for the study. Price changes for the companies receiving disclaimers and for their related industries were calculated at several dates covering three-month periods before and after issuance of the disclaimer. Comparison of company and industry price-change indexes produced no significant differences, leading the authors to conclude that either disclaimers are impounded by securities markets well before such reports are distributed publicly, or else disclaimers provide no relevant information.

In a comment that has special bearing for this study, the authors add: "If you would worry about the impact of [a disclaimer or any other 'unpleasant' form of audit opinion], concentrate instead on the individual reader of statements, whose reaction may be difficult to predict."

Kaplan (1978). Kaplan surveyed previous empirical research on the information content of financial accounting numbers. While primarily concerned with accounting reports and not auditors' reports, his review of research on interim or quarterly reports led him to conclude that "there is no evidence . . . that investors respond less strongly to quarterly reports than to annual reports, even though quarterly reports are unaudited." Such a statement raises doubts about the possible effect and value of the auditor's report.

Scott (1974). In this University of Illinois dissertation, Scott used the market model to investigate the information content of the auditor's consistency exception. His data suggest that the consistency disclosure does have information content for users and that they respond to such disclosures through their decisions.

Shank, Murdock, and Dillard (1977). A sample consisting of 268 firms that received *subject to* qualified audit opinions in 1973 or 1974 was matched with a control group on the basis of size, industry, and risk class (measured by average systematic risk). Market-price data were used to run tests on the change in systematic risk, or risk related to market-wide phenomena (the beta), change in the variance of the estimate of beta, and risk-adjusted security returns. The authors concluded that their results were consistent with the hypothesis that the capital market reacts to the audit-opinion form. They noted, however, that their methodology did not permit them to separate the effects of the underlying economic phenomenon on which the *subject to* qualification was based from the effects of the opinion form itself.

The problem of separating reaction to the form of the audit report from the underlying economic phenomena cannot be addressed adequately in a market-based study, but can be controlled in an experimental study. This point is developed in the discussion of research methodology used in the present study, chapter 4.

Experiments

Benjamin and Strawser (1974). Accounting students were used in an experiment to investigate the effects of auditors' reports on the compilation and assumptions (but not the accuracy) of forecasts. Earnings-per-share predictions were the dependent variable. Although 140 students participated, only ten were assigned to each treatment; thus results are based on comparisons in each case of two groups of ten subjects each. The auditor's report did make a difference (significant at the .05 level). Subjects that received financial statements and forecasts with an auditor's report predicted earnings per share for the next year at $1.34; when no audit report was presented the prediction was $1.20. Subjects were also asked to estimate a range within which the earnings per share would be likely to fall. If an auditor's report increases confidence in a forecast, we would expect that range predictions based at least partly on the forecast would be narrower than when no auditor's report is provided. This result did not occur; earnings-per-share range predictions were not significantly different.

Estes and Reimer (1977). Randomly selected bank loan officers were mailed a description of a hypothetical company plus a set of financial statements covering three years, with footnotes. A "benign" departure from generally accepted accounting principles was disclosed in a footnote. A test group received an auditor's opinion qualified for noncompliance with generally accepted accounting principles; a control group received a standard, unqualified opinion. Subjects were asked to indicate the maximum amount they would lend the company on a five-year mortgage note for the replacement of factory equipment, at 1½ percent over the prime interest-rate. The average loan response for the test group (120 loan officers) that received the qualified opinion was less than that of the control group (102 loan officers), but the difference was not statistically significant. The *except for* opinion form, considered separately from the information concerning the deviance from generally accepted accounting principles, did not significantly affect the bankers' decisions.

Estes and Reimer (1979). In this second study the same methodology and experimental package was used with chartered financial analysts, who were asked to indicate the price at which the company's common stock would represent an attractive investment. In this case the mean price response from the 108 members of the test group that received the qualified *except* *for* opinion was significantly less than that of the ninety-two analysts in the control group. The opinion form, apart from the information about the deviance from generally accepted accounting principles that was disclosed to both groups in a footnote, appears to have made a significant difference in the analysts' decisions.

Firth (1979). In an experiment similar to, but more extensive than that conducted by Estes and Reimer (1977), Firth tested the effects of a standard audit opinion compared to two versions of an opinion qualified for uncertainty and one qualified because of noncompliance with acceptable accounting principles (similar to *subject to* and *except for* qualifications in the United States). Subjects were bankers who were asked to examine financial statements and appended audit reports, and determine the maximum loan they would make to the hypothetical company. Two forms of the experiment were run with different groups, with consistent results. The audit report qualified for noncompliance with accounting principles produced no significant difference in loan amount; the reports qualified for uncertainty produced significant differences when compared with the standard report, and also when compared to the accounting principles qualification. Although the article is not altogether clear on this point, it appears that the bases for the uncertainty qualifications are revealed only in the audit reports, and not in the financial statements. Similarly, the fact that the inventory valuation method, which *is* disclosed in the statement notes, is not in compliance with acceptable accounting principles appears to be disclosed only in the audit report and not in the statements or notes. This is a subtle but significant point because it means that Firth has intermingled the unusual report forms with the economic factors giving rise to those forms. The significant differences obtained may be due, therefore, to the economic factors, the report form, or both.

Glazer (1978). In this University of Pennsylvania dissertation younger financial analysts in New York City were mailed an experimental package containing a basic set of financial-statement information, but varied as to (1) footnote disclosure of litigation uncertainties and (2) audit-opinion form. Fifty-two usable responses were received. The analysts were asked to estimate a return on investment for two investment alternatives, and to recommend allocation of the resources of a hypothetical client among these investment alternatives. Glazer's results indicate that the type and format of the auditor's report had no significant effect on participants' estimates of return on investment or resource-allocation recommendations.

Libby (1979b). In this experiment thirty-six bank officers from four banks in one city were used to test the effect of the *subject to* qualified auditor's opinion on responses as to (1) the rate premium over prime the bank would require to make a requested loan; (2) the rate premium the subject thought another bank would probably require; and (3) whether to make a loan or not. The uncertainty concerned pending litigation, and was disclosed in a footnote in all cases. No significant differences were obtained in responses when uncertainty was disclosed in a footnote with an unqualified audit opinion versus uncertainty disclosed in a footnote with an audit opinion qualified because of the uncertainty. Bertholdt (1979) and Schultz (1979) raised serious objections to the research partially because all the subjects were presented with an evaluation, identified as having been prepared by a senior bank officer, which was either very positive or very negative with respect to the probable litigation outcome. These reviewers felt that the management evaluation could override any other information source, including the auditor's opinion.

Reckers and Gramling (1979). An experiment was conducted by mail using ninety-five financial analysts as subjects. Each analyst was provided with a descriptive summary of a firm's recent history, a set of audited comparative financial statements, and a five-year-financial-highlights summary. A material lawsuit contingency was disclosed in a footnote, with some subjects receiving a package with a standard audit opinion, others receiving an unqualified opinion with a middle paragraph summarizing the footnote, and the remainder receiving an audit opinion that was qualified *subject to* the outcome of the uncertainty. The analysts were asked to forecast the firm's net earnings and stock price one year in the future. Tests of mean responses and standard deviations revealed no statistically significant differences among any of the pairs of disclosure forms, leading the authors to conclude that the *subject to* form of auditor qualification apparently has no information value.

Self-Assessment: Surveys and Interviews

Arthur Andersen & Co. (1974). When asked about the importance of an accountant's audit of financial statements in the valuation of securities, 88 percent of the 262 corporate executives interviewed and 90 percent of the 195 "key publics" indicated it was either very important or fairly important.

Chang and Most (1979). Individual investors, financial analysts, and institutional investors were surveyed in the United States, United Kingdom, and New Zealand. Respondents were asked to rate the importance of the income statement, balance sheet, statement of changes in financial position, accounting-policies statement, other footnotes, and auditor's report. The auditor's report was ranked fourth (ahead of the accounting-policies statement and other footnotes) by individual investors in the United Kingdom, next to last (ahead of other footnotes) by individual investors in New Zealand, and last by the other seven groups surveyed.

Corless and Norgaard (1974). This survey of financial analysts and MBA students, all located in Boston, New York, or Hartford, found that a CPA's report added little credibility to a forecasted statement of operations. The CPA's report would provide much greater confidence to 9 percent and slightly more confidence to 49 percent. Recall that the Benjamin and Strawser experiment (1974) found that an auditor's report accompanying a forecast did result in a significantly higher prediction of earnings per share, but no change in the predicted EPS range.

Guy, Greenway, Miller, and Mills (1974). Bank lending officers in Texas were surveyed by mail, with 159 responses. The officers were given examples of auditors' reports and asked to rate each in terms of the reliability it would lend to a set of financial statements. Rating was on a scale one to ten, with one indicating the highest reliability. The results were

Type of Audit Report	Mean Rating
Unqualified	1.4
Divided responsibility report (indicating that part of the examination was made by another auditor)	2.7
Qualified due to	
Lack of consistency	3.9
Omission of funds statement	4.2
Material uncertainty (*subject to* opinion)	5.6
Nonadherence to generally accepted accounting principles (*except for* opinion)	5.9
Adverse	6.6
Unaudited disclaimer	6.7

Among the report forms considered in the present study, the Guy et al. study did not include the disclaimer issued because of excessive uncertainty, or financial statements with no CPA report of any kind (financial statements with an "unaudited disclaimer" have not been audited, but are accompanied by a report from a CPA; some respondents in the Guy et al. study believed such a report lends reliability since "CPAs would not be associated with false or misleading statements").

One interesting result of this study is the small difference in ratings for the *subject to, except for,* and adverse opinions. In the eyes of Texas bankers one is about as bad as another, but all three are much worse than an unqualified opinion.

Lee and Tweedie (1977). The 301 United Kingdom shareholders interviewed ranked the auditor's report last among parts of the annual report, in terms of influence on investment decisions.

Stobie (1978). In an Australian mail survey, groups of financial-statement users were asked, "Does a qualified audit report have a significant effect on your willingness to invest in a particular company?" with the following results:

	n	*Yes*	*No*
Shareholders	60	85%	15%
Directors (managers)	76	82	18
Investment analysts	91	88	12

Respondents answering affirmatively gave these reasons (multiple responses were evidently allowed):

	Shareholders	*Directors*	*Analysts*
Because of the qualified report's:			
Effect on share prices	27%	22%	14%
Reflection on management's ability	45	50	45
Anticipated effect on potential sources of financing	22	25	23
Other	13	13	25

These results indicate that, at least in Australia, many users of financial statements believe a qualified audit opinion is a reflection on management's ability and may affect a company's share prices and its borrowing ability.

"What Bankers Think of CPA Services" (1974). In a survey of Michigan bankers, 91 percent said that it makes a difference whether a prospective borrower's financial statements have been "certified by a CPA." Respondents preferred "certified" financial statements because they are believed to be more reliable and not as self-serving as those not audited.

Winters (1975). In a study not directly concerned with the auditor's report, 566 bank loan officers indicated that a CPA's association with unaudited financial statements increased their degree of reliance on the statements greatly (17 percent) or somewhat (61 percent).

Experiments and market-based studies on the effects of audit reports are summarized in table 2-1. A few studies have concluded that certain forms

Table 2-1
Research Studies on the Effects of Audit Reports

Researcher	Opinion type	Data source	Effect
Alderman	Uncertainty qualification	Stock market	No significant effect
Firth	Uncertainty qualification	Stock market (U.K.)	Significant effect
Shank, Murdock, and Dillard	Uncertainty qualification	Stock market	Significant effect
Glazer	Uncertainty qualification	Financial analysts	No significant effect
Libby	Uncertainty qualification	Bankers	No significant effect
Reckers and Gramling	Uncertainty qualification	Financial analysts	No significant effect
Ball, Walker, and Whittred (Australia)	Noncompliance with GAAP	Stock market	Mixed
Estes and Reimer (1977)	Noncompliance with GAAP	Bankers	No significant effect
Estes and Reimer (1979)	Noncompliance with GAAP	Financial analysts	Significant effect
Firth	Noncompliance with GAAP	Stock market (U.K.)	No significant effect
Baskin	Consistency exception	Stock market	No significant effect
Scott	Consistency exception	Stock market	Significant effect
Firth	Adverse	Stock market (U.K.)	Significant effect
Frishkoff and Rogowski	Disclaimer	Stock market	No significant effect
Kaplan	Standard unqualified	Stock market	No significant effect (implied)
Benjamin and Strawser	Compilation of forecast	Accounting students	Significant effect

of the audit report produce a measurable and statistically significant effect on individual or aggregate investor behavior; other studies have found no such effect. The risk of Type II error, or erroneously accepting a null hypothesis by concluding that no significant difference exists between two statistics, is not evaluated in these studies. Indeed, evaluation of the risk of a Type II error requires information about population parameters that may be impossible to obtain in studies of investor behavior. Nevertheless, we can recognize that the probability of finding a significant effect is reduced when the variability of the population is large or the sample size is small. Human behavior appears to be highly variable, and the cost of obtaining a large sample, especially in an experimental study, can be great. While we must not ignore the evidence thus far accumulated, we should recognize that the tests in these studies may be too crude and insensitive to detect significant effects on human behavior even when they occur. Put another way, a significant difference is strong (although not conclusive) evidence; a difference that is not significant may be important evidence or it may be virtually meaningless, depending on the risk of a Type II error.

As for the other studies summarized here based on self-assessments by financial statement users, it appears that the audit report is important to bankers and financial analysts but not to shareholders (except perhaps in Australia); and CPA reports on forecasts add little credibility.

Summary

The most salient result of a comprehensive review of research on the auditor's report is this: despite substantial research effort, we still do not know with any degree of confidence the effect of the auditor's report on its intended audiences.

It appears that the report is not well read, especially by shareholders. Whether its presence and form are perceived when the report is not read is unknown. The auditor's role, the meaning of the audit report, and the type of report that will be rendered in particular circumstances are poorly understood by members of the business and financial community, although bankers and financial analysts are better informed than shareholders.

If the auditor's report is not read and, when read, is not fully understood, then we might be surprised if it were to have a significant and consistent effect on user behavior—and this pretty well summarizes the research on effect. Significant effects were found in a few studies, but these were outnumbered by studies in which no significant effects were found.

Communication, motivation, and decision making are complex; many valid and replicated studies are necessary before we begin to obtain reliable results. The auditor's report is part of a communication process that interacts with attitudes, personality characteristics, goals, decision processes, and other cues to produce (or not produce) behavioral effects. Twenty years ago fledgling accounting researchers may have hoped that one or two well-designed studies on any important question in accounting would produce valid and reliable results. If we have learned nothing else from the many research efforts during this period, we have learned that significant progress does not come so easily.

3

A Theoretical Perspective

In this chapter we look at the auditor's role and the auditor's report from the perspective of communication and human-information-processing theory, the conventional wisdom in accounting, and results of prior research. From this theoretical perspective, hypotheses are developed that form the basis for the research reported in the following chapters.

In his well-known work on the mathematical theory of communication, Weaver postulates the communication system represented in figure 3-1 (Shannon and Weaver 1964). He identifies three levels of problems in such a system:

Level A   How accurately can the symbols of communication be transmitted? (The technical problem)

Level B   How precisely do the transmitted symbols convey the desired meaning? (The semantic problem)

Level C   How effectively does the received meaning affect conduct in the desired way? (The effectiveness problem)

The technical problem is important in electronic communication but is of little concern in considering the auditor's report.

The semantic problem is of considerably greater concern, and much effort has been expended by the accounting profession to develop report wording that effectively conveys specific meaning. This effort has been frustrated and frustrating. The variety of circumstances that reports must cover, coupled with the range of experience and competence among CPAs, could produce a broad variety of reports. Consequently, the profession opted for a small number of permissable report forms, but this decision restricted CPAs in their ability to accurately and precisely encode the meaning they would convey to receivers and has not produced the intended consistency. Research by Dillard, Murdock, and Shank (1978) reveals substantial disagreement among CPAs in their choice of opinion forms that should be used and the messages that should be conveyed even in fairly well-defined circumstances. Only 53 percent of the CPAs participating in their study agreed with the disclosure and opinion form actually used by other CPAs in a selected set of cases.

The accounting profession's efforts toward standardization of report forms and terminology may have resulted in a set of specialized symbols

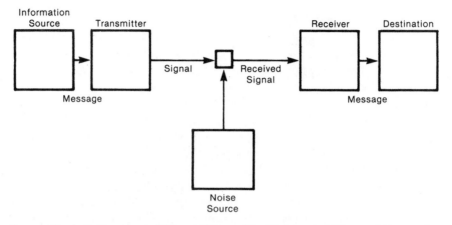

Figure 3-1. A Communication-System Model

and phrases that can be fully understood only by one who has undertaken special study. In discussing the *except for* and *subject to* opinion forms, Carmichael (1972, p. 86) suggests, "The full impact of the distinction cannot be known to a report reader unless he has read AICPA pronouncements on reporting," and adds, "Few average readers probably have any facility in distinguishing the niceties of expression used in modification of the standard short-form report." Carmichael is pointing to the likelihood of an effectiveness problem. Report readers may not be able to understand or interpret the report phrases and form as intended by the auditor.

Glazer (1978) synthesizes human information processing theories in the simplified model presented in figure 3-2. The auditor's report, or some part of it, is received by the financial-statement user as a distal stimulus or cue. Through the user's perceptual, motivation, and memory subsystems distal stimuli are formed into interpretations, or proximal stimuli, which are then melded into concepts and judgments. Based upon this information processing, a response is made by the user which may range from a decision to purchase stock to a change in belief structure (for example, an assessment of management's ability or a prediction of the next period's earnings).

The effectiveness of communication, in the sense of producing desired behavior outcomes, is a function not only of encoding and transmission, but also of every aspect of human information processing on the receiver's end. Examination of each of these aspects is beyond the scope of the present study, but it may be useful to focus on the four relevant cue dimensions identified by Glazer:

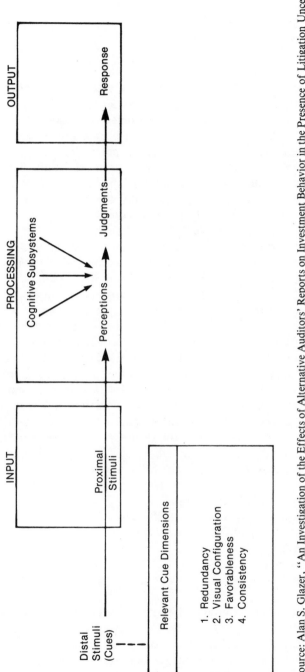

Source: Alan S. Glazer, "An Investigation of the Effects of Alternative Auditors' Reports on Investment Behavior in the Presence of Litigation Uncer-tainties." Ph.D. diss. (Philadelphia: University of Pennsylvania, 1978), p. 35. Reprinted with permission.

Figure 3-2. A Model of Human Information Processing

1. Redundancy
2. Visual configuration
3. Favorableness
4. Consistency

Redundancy provides emphasis and increases the likelihood that a cue will have an effect on behavior (Glazer, pp. 50-51). Redundancy may occur between the auditor's report and the body of financial statements or financial-statement footnotes. It will occur between the opinion paragraph of a qualified opinion and the middle paragraph where the issue is elaborated. Some redundancy may be present in the standard opinion, with references to the financial statements in both the scope and the opinion paragraphs, and use of the term "generally accepted" in both paragraphs.

Research on the role of shapes and patterns in concept formation has been inconclusive (Glazer, p. 55). Nevertheless, anecdotal evidence in accounting supports the notion that the visual configuration of the auditor's report—that is, its length and number of paragraphs—significantly affects its interpretation. This notion was the basis for the *Wall Street Journal* headline of April 17, 1975: "If Auditor's Opinion Runs 3 Paragraphs, Take Heed."

The perceived favorableness of a cue may also affect its interpretation and its weight in impression formation. In particular, negative cues appear to receive more weight than favorable cues (Glazer, pp. 57-58). This would suggest that an audit opinion that was perceived as negative or unfavorable would have a greater effect on user response than one viewed as neutral or favorable. Carmichael (1972, p. 2) believes that audit opinions can be ordered on some sort of favorableness scale: "A financial statement user, in making his resource allocation decision, places less reliance on the financial statements in correspondence to the degree to which the audit opinion is qualified." Similarly, Anderson, Giese, and Booker (1970, p. 525) rank opinions, from best to worst, in the following order:

1. The clean or standard opinion
2. The opinion with a scope qualification
3. The *except for* qualified opinion
4. The *subject to* opinion
5. The disclaimer
6. The adverse opinion

Anderson, Giese, and Booker offer no research evidence supporting this ranking, and the Committee on Basic Auditing Concepts (1973, p. 45) of the American Accounting Association expresses doubt: "The correspondence of each of these grades of opinion with degrees of credibility is clear neither for the auditor nor for his user audience."

The perceived consistency among cues may affect their interpretation. Consistency can operate in the same way as redundancy, reinforcing the effect of a cue. Inconsistency can create dissonance and rejection of both cues, or acceptance of the one that reinforces a preferred judgment. Research has found that inconsistency between a powerful and a less powerful cue tends to produce discounting of the less powerful (Glazer, p. 59). If the auditor's report appears to be inconsistent with other cues, such as the company president's letter or financial-statement footnotes, the cue that appears to be the less powerful, perhaps because of more conservative language, may be discounted.

Except for a few researchers such as Glazer, accountants have not studied the structure and workings of human information-processing systems but have nevertheless been willing to pronounce upon the effects of cues such as financial statements and auditor's reports in those systems. Thus the accounting literature is replete with assertions about the role, impact, and effect of the audit report on user behavior. A few examples will illustrate this conventional wisdom.

> . . . the audit profession fills a social need by reporting on the reliability of financial information. (Carmichael 1972, p. 2)

> The attest function in the United States and other highly industrialized nations of the free world serves an essential purpose in modern society by adding credibility to financial and other economic data via the measurement, substantiation and communication processes. (Bevis 1962, p. 35)

> The independent auditor's role is to enhance the credibility of financial information. By performing that role, independent auditors further the operation of an effective capital market. (Carmichael 1974, p. 64)

> . . . the application of the auditing process to the communication of accounting information enhances the value of accounting information . . . .

> The audit function adds to the *credibility* of information because the user can have confidence that the types of controls indicated above are present in the communication process. . . .

> The audit report, the end-product of the auditor's efforts, is intended to facilitate this communication [of economic information] by adding credibility to the information reported, to the extent it is believed to be justified. (Committee on Basic Auditing Concepts 1973, pp. 8, 13, 41)

> The assurances provided by an audit hold significant information value for users of financial statements. For example, knowledge that an audit has been performed is normally assumed to affect an entity's cost of obtaining funds. (Commission on Auditors' Responsibilities 1978, p.6)

> If capital is to flow freely and efficiently in our free enterprise economy, the consumers of financial information must continue to have full con-

fidence in the product they receive. Independent auditors play a crucial role in maintaining this public confidence. (Kapnick 1978, p. 1)

While these views from within the accounting profession may be biased and even self-indulgent, they are supported by the Credit Research Foundation:

> Basically, it is the auditor's report which accompanies the balance sheet and income statements that gives them value and meaning. . . .
>
> The advantage to the credit grantor in having an acceptable CPA on the books is that the risk is improved. (Arminio 1970, pp. 45, 51)

There are those, however, who take a contrary position:

> The external audit is not of obvious value to either management or shareholders and there is much questioning of both the cost of this function and the manner in which it is performed. (Briston and Perks 1977, p. 48)

But dissenters are a minority, and the conventional wisdom is that the auditor's report adds credibility to financial statements and reduces the risk of relying on them.

The communication model, human information-processing theory, and the conventional wisdom can be related to prior research through the probabilistic communications flow chart presented in figure 3-3.

Following an examination of financial statements, the auditor determines the message he would like the report reader to receive. This message must be encoded within a limited number of opinion forms; wording for any middle paragraph is less limited but still constrained. If CPAs were to agree on the message to be communicated for given circumstances, they might still disagree on the report form and content to be used (how the message is to be encoded). Evidence from prior research indicates the probability of agreement for one set of cases is only about 53 percent (Dillard, Murdock, and Shank 1978). For illustrative purposes let us assume that P_1, the probability that the encoded message will accurately reflect the auditor's intended meaning, is .60.

Although transmission can occur in several ways, the most common means of transmission of the auditor's message to financial-statement users is through a printed annual report. CPAs carefully check printers' proofs and subsequently verify that the audit opinion distributed as part of the annual report agrees with the opinion originally issued. Thus the probability of accurate transmission through this medium is close to 1.00. The auditor's message is also transmitted through other media. Qualified audit opinions may be mentioned in the financial press. Investors may not examine the annual report, but may rely instead on information obtained from brokers, financial services, friends, and similar sources. These sources will rarely

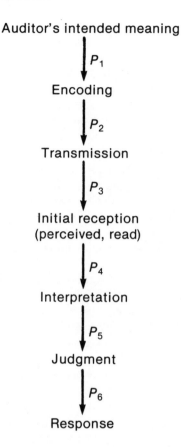

Auditor's intended meaning

P_1

Encoding

P_2

Transmission

P_3

Initial reception
(perceived, read)

P_4

Interpretation

P_5

Judgment

P_6

Response

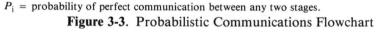

P_i = probability of perfect communication between any two stages.

Figure 3-3. Probabilistic Communications Flowchart

communicate the entire auditor's message, and may misstate it in large or small degree. Allowing for transmission errors in media other than the annual report, the transmission probability, P_2, may be estimated at about .95.

The investor has freedom to choose whether to receive the auditor's message or not. A minimum list of choices would include:

1. Failing to see the auditor's opinion, by avoiding its page in an annual report or by ignoring the annual report altogether.
2. Perceiving the presence of an opinion, perhaps by seeing its identifying caption, with no further attention. In this case the investor may be aware that an audit was performed (although a knowledgeable investor

will often assume that an audit was performed simply because the company is listed on a securities exchange, whether or not the opinion is seen).

3. Perceiving the presence and physical configuration (length, number of paragraphs) of the audit report. Some communication occurs here, since a standard, short-form report has a distinct, two-paragraph form. When three or more paragraphs are present, the reader may realize that something has been explained but cannot know whether the opinion has been qualified without actually reading a part of it.
4. Identifying the type of report, such as a *subject to* qualification. This requires at least some reading of the first line of the opinion paragraph.
5. Determining the general cause for any qualification. This may be accomplished by scanning the middle paragraph.
6. Reading the report carefully one or more times, and probably referring to any cited parts of the financial statements or footnotes.

As noted in chapter 2, several studies have investigated the readership of the auditor's report. Shareholders reporting they never read the report range from 2 to 33 percent in the United States, and up to 48 percent in the United Kingdom. When "rarely" and "never" categories are added together, the range in the United States is 14 to 58 percent for shareholders, and 13 to 37 percent for professional investors. The investor's reception choice probably depends upon many factors, including the recent behavior of the stock market, events affecting the particular company, and personal characteristics; this variability might account for the range of research results. To continue our illustration, we will assume that 75 percent of the investors who receive an audit report read or perceive it sufficiently for the intended message to get through; $P_3 = .75$.

Once a message is technically received, or passes the receiver's senses, its content and meaning must be interpreted. If investors are not familiar with the nature and purpose of financial statement audits, interpretation is liable to be imperfect. Research reveals several problems with understanding of the audit function:

1. Over one-third of the shareowners in a major survey believe that all financial records are examined in a financial-statement audit (Arthur Andersen & Co. 1974). In a South African study, about the same proportion of shareholders and 14 percent of investment analysts held this erroneous belief (Stobie 1978).
2. Two-thirds of responding shareowners and over one-half of responding analysts and brokers think that the most important function of an audit is to detect significant fraud (Arthur Andersen & Co.). The proportion of shareowners who hold this view is even higher in the United Kingdom

(Lee 1970) and Australia (Beck 1973), but only 33 percent in South Africa (Stobie).

3. Substantial numbers of shareholders in the United Kingdom (Lee), Australia (Beck), and South Africa (Stobie) think the audit report provides assurance that management is efficient and that the company is sound.

The different report forms are also a source of misunderstanding. Carmichael questions whether the average report reader distinguishes between the *except for* and the *subject to* forms of qualification (1972, p. 86), but also thinks that financial-statement users place less reliance on qualified opinions (p. 2). An early study indicates that CPAs do not think their clients' bankers clearly understand the differences between an unqualified opinion, a qualified opinion, and a disclaimer (Ashworth 1963). And when asked to identify the form of opinion that should have been issued in particular cases, less than half the bankers, financial analysts, and corporate financial officers selected the form that was actually used by the CPA (Shank, Dillard, and Murdock 1977 and 1978; Shank, Dillard, and Bylinski 1979). Briloff (1966) also found disagreement over opinion form.

Terms and phrases within the auditor's report can be a source of misunderstanding. Bennett (1976) studied three key phrases in the opinion paragraph and concluded that their meanings were significantly different among stockholders, management accountants, and public accountants with CPA firms. Similar results were obtained by Briloff (1966), but Oliver (1974), in studying mainly accounting terms as opposed to audit opinion terms, found a "communication base" between CPAs and report users.

Research into overall understanding of the audit report has produced mixed results. Libby (1979a) suggested that "fears of miscommunication of the messages intended by audit reports to more sophisticated users may not be justified"; his studies involved bank lending officers. Most responding shareholders (85 percent), bankers (99 percent), and financial analysts (95 percent) told Fess and Ziegler (1977) that they understand the auditor's report completely or understand most of it. But in another study, 22 percent of the shareholders in the United States say they have difficulty understanding the auditor's report (Epstein 1975), and researchers in the United Kingdom concluded that 39 percent of shareholders in that country have no understanding of the auditor's report (Lee and Tweedie 1977).

Given accurate reception of the intended message, what is the probability, P_4, of a correct interpretation. Research evidence is mixed, and probably indicates that interpretation is a function of personal knowledge, experience, interest, and similar factors. But since self-assessments of understanding may be overly optimistic, we would probably not be far off if we assigned a value to P_4 of .75.

Applying the rule of joint probabilities, we might roughly estimate the likelihood of a correct interpretation of the auditor's original intended meaning as:

$$P_1 \times P_2 \times P_3 \times P_4 = .60 \times .95 \times .75 \times .75 = .32$$

Given the limited choice of report forms and phrasing constraints, transmission problems, failure of investors to read or even see the report, and misunderstandings of function and meaning, our assumed values indicate that the receiver has only about one chance in three of receiving and interpreting the auditor's intended meaning correctly.

While accountants have been willing to state, on the basis of their beliefs and wishes, the effect of the auditor's report on its audiences, they have been silent about the intended response. An American Accounting Association committee may be unique in its attention to this question:

> The auditor needs to ponder the question, "What do I want to have happen as the result of this message?" A primary purpose of communication is to influence or affect the behavior of the receiver. If the auditor is not clear as to what he wishes the receiver to do or not do as the result of his message, he may not only fail in his purpose to gain the desired effect but, instead, cause the reverse to happen. (Committee on Basic Auditing Concepts 1973, p. 51)

The lack of authoritative statements or even speculation on the desired response may mean that the auditor actually has no desired response in mind, but intends only to provide the user with information which the user may deal with as he or she wishes. If this interpretation is correct, then the auditor would be neutral toward user judgments such as the following:

> "These financial statements are not accompanied by an audit report, but I'm going to assume they have been audited anyway and are accurate."

> "This *subject to* opinion means the company is in big trouble and is a poor investment."

> "The auditor is taking exception with the statements; this probably means that fraud has occurred, and that management is crooked."

> "A disclaimer means the company stinks, and the auditor won't go near them. Certainly not a good investment."

> "A qualified opinion is issued when the auditor and management can't agree, and indicates management is not very competent."

In fact, most auditors would probably prefer that none of these judgments occur, but failure to consider intended outcomes makes these and equally unfortunate results possible.

For the sake of extending our consideration of probabilities, let us assume that a desired outcome does exist in the mind of the auditor. After the report is interpreted by the receiver, it will be combined with other information to form a judgment. Whether this judgment will conform to that desired by the auditor will depend on the receiver's access to other relevant sources of information and his effective integration of that information with his interpretation of the audit report. Let us give this probability, P_5, a (probably generous) value of .80.

Execution of the desired response requires the selection and application of an optimal decision model, such as a net present value model when future amounts are involved. Conservatively, the probability of such an optimal selection, or P_6, is not likely to exceed .85.

Assuming the auditor has a desired outcome, its likelihood of occurrence in our hypothetical case is now:

$$P_1 \times P_2 \times P_3 \times P_4 \times P_5 \times P_6 = .60 \times .95 \times .75 \times .75 \times .80 \times .85 = .22$$

Given our probably conservative assumptions, there is less than one chance in four that the desired outcome will occur. In other words, all the efforts and costs that go into audit reports may be incurred for a 22 percent chance of producing desired results!

This analysis indicates that we should expect little demonstrated effect from audit reports. Table 2-1 shows that, in the market-based and experimental research to date, nine studies produced no significant effect attributable to audit-report variations, six showed a significant effect, and one produced mixed results. These research results are quite in line with what our analysis leads us to expect.

Our discussion to this point has dealt only with external communication between the auditor and users of financial statements, and possible resulting effects. A financial-statement audit may be valuable even in the absence of any external effects, if it induces company management to establish adequate accounting controls and to comply with acceptable accounting principles in the first place. As noted by Ng (1979, p. 105), any errors discovered during the audit will be corrected; further, managers are less likely to bias their reports if they know that they will be audited. The Commission on Auditors' Responsibilities (1978, pp. 6-7) supports Ng's view: "An audit has a value independent of what users may derive from the information audited" due to the improvement in the entity's accountability. Notwithstanding this possible internal value of a financial statement audit, ". . . the primary beneficiary of the audit process is the *user* of the accounting information'' (Committee on Basic Auditing Concepts 1973, p. 8), and the remaining focus of the present study will consequently be on the effects on external users.

The foregoing theoretical perspective suggests the following research hypotheses:

H_1 The addition of a standard audit report to a set of financial statements will significantly affect investor behavior.

H_2 The effects on investor behavior of the several nonstandard audit report forms will differ significantly from the effects of the standard audit-report form.

These hypotheses are restated more explicitly and in null form in the next chapter.

Research Design

Researchers investigating the effects of the auditor's report on investor behavior have essentially two methodological choices: analysis of market data or controlled experiments. Market-based studies use data that reflect actual investor decisions and are thus superior on the dimension of realism, but they have several disadvantages:

1. The date of impact is difficult to identify—the date when financial-statement users actually read the auditor's opinion. This date will differ from the date of the opinion, and may differ from the date statements are released.

2. Market-based studies are restricted to analysis of aggregated data, such as number of shares traded, total value of trades, and average price; decisions and attitudes of individuals, and the rationales behind them, cannot be investigated directly. This point was underscored by Frishkoff and Rogowski (1978, p. 57) in the conclusion to their report on a market-based study. They suggested that management should not be concerned with the impact of a nonstandard audit-report on their firm's securities prices, since this impact is likely to be negligible and is, at any rate, not controllable; they recommended that management instead concentrate on the individual user of financial statements, whose reaction is likely to be more difficult to predict.

3. Only a limited number of opinion forms are generally released for companies listed on securities exchanges: the standard opinion and opinions qualified because of scope limitation, uncertainty, or lack of consistency. Other opinion forms are issued too infrequently to provide an adequate basis for statistical analysis.

4. Market-based studies cannot investigate the effects of specific-opinion form separately from the effects of the factors that give rise to an opinion. For example, when an opinion is qualified because of uncertainty, information about the uncertainty must be included in footnotes to the financial statements. Market-data analysis can investigate the effects of the uncertainty on decisions, but cannot investigate the effects of the qualified-opinion form separately from that uncertainty.

5. Similarly, market-data analysis cannot study the differential effect of an audit and the auditor's standard report on user's of financial statements; since listed companies must be audited, a control group of unaudited statements is not available. A control group receiving unaudited

statements could be identified, at considerable expense, among bank lending officers, but not among investors. The experimental approach is more practical for studying the effect of audited versus unaudited statements, and is the only practical method available for studying the effect on investors. For these reasons, a behavioral-field-experiment methodology was chosen for the present study to investigate the effects of an audit and of different audit-opinion forms on investor behavior.

Although he raised questions concerning response measurement, Carmichael (1972, p. 163) endorsed an experimental approach:

> To study the decision process of financial statement users and retain control over the relevant variables, an experimental simulation or a laboratory experiment would seem to be the most logical choice for a data-collection setting.

An experimental approach was further indicated because of the impracticality of obtaining a large and representative sample of actual, individual investment decisions and attitudinal measures while simultaneously controlling for the extraneous variables and personal characteristics that might impact the response measures.

The Posttest-Only-Control-Group Experimental Design

The posttest-only-control-group experimental design was selected as most appropriate for the present study. This design was strongly endorsed by Campbell and Stanley (1963) in their cardinal work on experimentation, and has the following form:

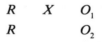

$$R \quad X \quad O_1$$
$$R \qquad\quad O_2$$

where: R represents random assignment of subjects
X represents the experimental treatment
O represents observation on the subjects

Subjects are first randomly assigned to control and test groups, an experimental stimulus or treatment is applied to the test group, and observations are then taken on both groups. This design was used to test hypotheses concerning the presence or absence of a standard auditor's opinion, and was expanded to the following multiple test group design to investigate the effects of the *except for*, *subject to*, adverse, and disclaimer report forms:

$$R \quad X_1 \quad O_1$$
$$R \quad X_2 \quad O_2$$
$$R \quad X_3 \quad O_3$$
$$R \quad X_4 \quad O_4$$
$$R \qquad\quad\; O_5$$

The design does not permit pretesting of subjects to establish equivalence between the control and test groups, but is, nevertheless, supported by Campbell and Stanley on the grounds that randomization provides the best assurance of lack of initial biases between groups. In this study, professional investor and shareholder subjects were randomly selected, and all subjects, including those in the general business category, were randomly assigned to groups. But, as discussed later, a significantly greater effort was also made to deal with subject differences by obtaining measurements on a number of personal characteristics and controlling for these statistically.

Campbell and Stanley (1963, pp. 175-176) identify the following twelve factors that may jeopardize the validity of various experimental designs:

1. Factors threatening internal validity (variables that, if not controlled in the experimental design, might produce effects confounded with the effect of the experimental stimulus):

A. History—The events that might occur between the first and second measurement, other than the experimental variable. Only one measurement is taken in the posttest-only design, so no events can intervene.
B. Maturation—Processes internal to the respondents that operate in response to the passage of time (not specific to the particular events), such as aging, tiring, or becoming hungrier. Maturation was not a factor for the general business-person group since treatment and response occurred within a span of minutes. This was very probably the case for shareholders and professional investors, but we cannot be certain. It would have been unusual for a subject to read the material, put it aside for some period of time, and then complete the response form without rereading the material—unusual, but not impossible. The maturation factor is at best a minimal threat in the posttest-only design as applied, but not controlled for completely.
C. Testing—The conditioning effect of the first exposure to a test on the score of a second testing. Only one "test" was administered, so this factor is not a threat.
D. Instrumentation—The possible effects on measurements of changes in the measuring instruments or in the persons taking the measurements. As the present experiment was structured, no such changes could occur.

E. Statistical regression—Can occur when selection of groups is based on their extreme scores. Selection was not made on such a basis in this study.

F. Selection bias—Resulting from the use of different selection criteria or approaches for the comparison groups. Subjects were randomly assigned to control and test groups; while this does not assure equivalence among the groups, it does prevent selection bias.

G. Experimental mortality—Or loss of respondents at a rate different from the comparison groups. Since stimulus and response occurred within a very short time, usually a matter of minutes, mortality is not a problem in the present study.

H. Selection-maturation interaction—Might be confounded with and mistaken for the effect of the experimental variable. Since selection bias was prevented by random assignment, selection bias is not present to interact with any possible maturation (maturation was also very unlikely).

2. Factors threatening external validity or the representativeness of results:

A. The reactive or interaction effect of testing—In which a pretest might affect a participant's sensitivity to the experimental variable. Pretests were not used in these experiments.

B. The interaction effects of selection biases and the experimental variable—Selection bias was avoided through random assignment of subjects to control and treatment groups.

C. Reactive effects of experimental arrangements—Make it impossible to generalize about the effects of the experimental variable on persons encountering it in nonexperimental settings. This effect cannot be fully controlled in any experiment, and is in fact the objection to experimental studies in accounting that is most frequently cited. It is, essentially, a weakness that must be accepted with the experimental approach, but can be controlled to a degree by increasing the realism of the experimental task.

D. Multiple-treatment interference—The effect on subjects of multiple treatments due to the possibility that the effects of prior treatments are remembered or not perfectly eliminated. While several treatments are tested in the present study, this problem does not apply because each subject is exposed to only one treatment.

As can be seen from the preceding discussion, the posttest-only-control-group experimental design permits control over all of the internal threats to validity and, as applied in the present study, all but one of the external threats. Of the three preexperimental designs and the three true experimental designs discussed by Campbell and Stanley, the posttest-only-control-group design allows for the greatest control over factors threatening internal and external validity.

The experimental materials are reproduced in appendix A, and are discussed in the following sections.

Independent Variables

If we administer a stimulus to one person, then take some response measurement for this person and for another person, we could not be sure that any difference in responses was due to the stimulus. It could be due to differences between the two individuals. One could be more intelligent, or older, or wealthier, or angrier than the other. One approach to control for such differences is to match subjects on the basis of measured characteristics. Another approach, much simpler and in many cases infinitely more practical, is to seek subject equivalence through random assignment to control and treatment groups. This approach is, as noted earlier, recommended by Campbell and Stanley. Random assignment was used in the present experiment, but human behavior and especially investment behavior appear to be so variable among individuals that extra assurance of equivalence was sought by controlling for several personal characteristics. This control is achieved by measuring each subject on the several control variables and then statistically removing the effect of each variable from the dependent variables (decisions, attitudes, and so on).

Elias (1972) controlled for nine background variables in an experiment concerned with the effects of human asset accounting. These were

1. Familiarity with human-asset accounting
2. Length of business experience
3. Level of education
4. Recency of education
5. Number of college-level courses completed in accounting and finance
6. Age
7. Experience with buying or selling common stock other than as part of job duties
8. The degree to which consulting or advising investors constitutes part of the job
9. Degree of interest in the social sciences

None of these variables had a significant effect on Elias's investment decision, except for number 8 under one treatment.

In a related study Hendricks (1976) controlled for a similar set of background variables:

1. Age
2. Number of courses completed in accounting and finance
3. Number of years of business experience
4. Employment status
5. The extent to which advising investors or evaluating stocks is part of the job
6. Number of personal stock transactions completed
7. The number of human-asset articles read
8. The number of human-asset-accounting lectures or class meetings attended
9. Score on the Short-Form Dogmatism Scale

The dogmatism score was added in apparent response to criticism of Elias for his failure to control for the openness or closedness of belief systems. Of these nine variables only number 3, the number of years of business experience, was found to be significantly correlated (after partialling out the effects of each other control variable) with the stock-investment decision, the dependent variable.

Hull (1980) similarly found no significant effect on investment decisions from degree of education, experience, or information-processing style.

In their review of prior research on the use of students as surrogates in behavioral-accounting research, Ashton and Kramer (1980) suggest that differences in responses between students and nonstudents might be largely explained by differences in age, experience, and wealth.

Several of these background variables were included in the present study despite their failure to produce significant effects in the Elias, Hendricks, and Hull studies, in order to investigate in a different context and with different subjects their possible effects on decisions and attitudes and to control for any such effects. Original control variables were also developed for this study. Responses were obtained from subjects on the following variables (see the response form in appendix A for precise wording):

1. EXPERIENCE—years of business experience
2. ACCOUNTING HOURS—credit hours in accounting courses
3. FINANCE HOURS—credit hours in finance and investment courses
4. YEARS OF COLLEGE—years of college work completed
5. MARKET VALUE OF STOCKS—approximate market value of investments in corporate stocks
6. MARKET VALUE OF BONDS—approximate market value of investments in corporate bonds

7. OTHER INVESTMENTS—approximate market value of other securities including government bonds, savings accounts, certificates of deposits, etcetera.
8. STOCK TRANSACTIONS—approximate number of stock transactions executed within the past two years
9. STOCK EVALUATIONS—subject was asked to indicate how frequently he evaluates stocks or advises investors
10. SEX
11. AGE
12. DJIA ESTIMATE—subject's estimate of the current closing Dow Jones Industrial Average
13. ACTUAL DJIA—subjects indicated the date of their participation in the experiment; this date was translated into the closing DJIA and compared with the DJIA ESTIMATE (above) as a measure of familiarity with the stock market
14. INVESTMENT ATTITUDE—subjects indicated agreement or disagreement on a five-point-Likert-type scale with the statement, "This is a good time to be investing in the stock market."

Variables 1-11 were inspired by and have been used in other studies. The DJIA ESTIMATE was added to permit additional control over differential market familiarity among subjects. The ACTUAL DJIA was recorded for two purposes: for comparison with the estimate, to obtain a difference representing lack of familiarity; and, since subjects would not all complete the response form on the same day, to partially control for the effects of changing market conditions on subject behavior. The INVESTMENT ATTITUDE variable was likewise added for two reasons: to control for different investment philosophies among subjects; and to capture, and thus control for, part of the effect of changes in the investment climate.

Dependent Variables

Investor behavior culminates in a decision, such as to invest in a certain security at or below a certain price, to sell a certain number of units, to continue holding a security, and to not invest in a given security. In general, the procedure that produces the decision, the decision model, consists of six stages: (1) identification of an objective; (2) identification of a set of alternative courses of action; (3) estimation or projection of an outcome, in terms of objective attainment, for each alternative; (4) estimation of the likelihood of each outcome; (5) selection of an alternative (the decision); and (6) implementation of the decision. (See Horngren 1977, chapter 24 for a typical discussion.) The result of decision implementation is reflected, in the aggregate, in stock market data used in the market-based studies discussed in chapter 2. In an experimental context it is possible to go behind this final consequence to examine intermediate results in the decision process. For this study four responses were developed to measure some of the projections and estimates investors may develop prior to reaching a decision (step 3 in the decision process):

A. INCOME PROJECTION—estimate of next year's net income for the J Company, in thousands of dollars (000 omitted). Reckers and Gramling (1979) used a similar variable in their study of the effect of the *subject to* opinion, and concluded that the opinion form had no significant effect on the income projection.

B. SHARE-PRICE ESTIMATE—estimate of a fair price per share for J Company common stock. Reckers and Gramling, in an experiment using chartered financial analysts, found that the *subject to* audit opinion produced no significant difference in share price estimates. In a similar experiment Estes and Reimer (1979) found that the *except for* opinion form did produce a significant reduction in estimates of a fair price for a company's shares. And a study sponsored by Arthur Andersen & Co. (1974) found that a majority of executives and other "key publics" interviewed considered the auditing of financial statements to be "very important" in the valuation of securities.

C. COMPANY EVALUATION—agreement or disagreement with a statement that the J Company is successful. Previous studies in Australia (Beck 1973), South Africa (Stobie 1978), and the United Kingdom (Lee 1970), where audit procedures and reports are similar to those in the United States, indicate that many shareholders and other financial statement users expect the auditor's report to provide assurance concerning the efficiency and soundness of the company.

D. MANAGEMENT EVALUATION—agreement or disagreement that J Company's management is well qualified. The studies by Beck, Stobie, and Lee found that substantial numbers of financial-statement users expect the auditor's report to provide assurance that management is efficient.

Subjects were also required to make a decision (step 5 in the decision process discussed above):

E. INVESTMENT DECISION—out of a fund balance of $100,000 that must be immediately and fully invested in New York Stock Exchange listed companies, the amount the subject would invest in the J Company (fund structure and objective were also given). Glazer's (1978) experiment indicated that the type and format of auditor's report had no significant effect on investment allocations between two alternatives.

On the other hand, in an Australian survey by Stobie (1978) responses were overwhelmingly positive to the question, "Does a qualified audit report have a significant effect on your willingness to invest in a particular company?"

Two other responses were obtained to measure effects that are related to, but are not so obviously a part of the decision model:

F. CONFIDENCE RATING—self-assessment of the subject's confidence in his/her investment decision. According to the American Accounting Association's Committee on Basic Auditing Concepts (1973), the information user "will be more confident in using the information for its intended purpose than he would be if the audit function had not been performed."

G. ASSESSMENT OF FRAUD—agreement or disagreement with a statement about the risk of fraud in J Company. Several earlier studies (Beck 1973; Lee 1970; Arthur Andersen & Co. 1974; Stobie, 1978) found that statement users believe the audit will prevent or detect fraud, and that the audit report provides assurance that fraud has not occurred.

As noted in chapter 3, the conventional wisdom holds that the auditor's report should increase investor confidence in financial statements. If this is so, then it should also increase investor confidence in decisions they make in reliance upon financial statements. The CONFIDENCE RATING variable allows this proposition to be investigated.

Previous studies, especially in the United Kingdom (see chapter 2), have found that many stockholders believe an independent audit is undertaken to prevent or find fraud. A stockholder holding this view should be reassured concerning the risk of fraud by the presence of an audit opinion on a company's financial statements. The ASSESSMENT OF FRAUD variable was included to test this hypothesis.

Variables actually used in the subsequent regression analysis (some of the control variables proved to be insignificant) are listed for reference in appendix B.

The Experimental Packet

Financial data were developed for the hypothetical J Company based on averages for the household-appliance industry, adjusted to meet several criteria for normalcy. The objective was to provide financial statements with no extremes or "red flags" to distort responses. The same company description, financial statements, five-year statistical summary, and statement footnotes were provided to each subject. The page containing the footnotes was printed with one of the following audit-opinion versions:

1. No auditor's opinion; footnotes centered on the page to avoid calling attention to this fact (control group for the standard opinion).

2. Standard opinion:

   We have examined the consolidated balance sheets of J Company as of December 31, 19X5 and 19X4 and the statements of consolidated income, retained earnings, and changes in financial position for the years then ended. Our examinations were made in accordance with generally accepted auditing standards and, accordingly, included such tests of the accounting records and such other auditing procedures as we considered necessary in the circumstances.

   In our opinion, the financial statements referred to above present fairly the consolidated financial position of J Company as of December 31, 19X5 and 19X4 and the consolidated results of its operations and the changes in its financial position for the years then ended, in conformity with generally accepted accounting principles applied on a consistent basis.

3. Standard opinion with middle paragraph (control group for the remaining four opinion forms):

   We have examined the consolidated balance sheets of J Company as of December 31, 19X5 and 19X4 and the statements of consolidated income, retained earnings, and changes in financial position for the years then ended. Our examinations were made in accordance with generally accepted auditing standards and, accordingly, included such tests of the accounting records and such other auditing procedures as we considered necessary in the circumstances.

   During the current year the Company became a defendant in a lawsuit alleging infringement of certain patent rights and claiming royalties and punitive damages. The Company has filed a counter action, and preliminary hearings and discovery proceedings on both actions are in progress. Company officers and counsel believe the Company has a good chance of prevailing, but the ultimate outcome of the lawsuits cannot presently be determined. No provision for any liability that may result has been made in the financial statements, nor do the financial statements contain any disclosure of this matter.

   In our opinion, the financial statements referred to above present fairly the consolidated financial position of J Company as of December 31, 19X5 and 19X4 and the consolidated results of its operations and the changes in its financial position for the years then ended, in conformity with generally accepted accounting principles applied on a consistent basis.

4. *Except for* qualified opinion:

We have examined the consolidated balance sheets of J Company as of December 31, 19X5 and 19X4 and the statements of consolidated income, retained earnings, and changes in financial position for the years then ended. Our examinations were made in accordance with generally accepted auditing standards and, accordingly, included such tests of the accounting records and such other auditing procedures as we considered necessary in the circumstances.

During the current year the Company became a defendant in a lawsuit alleging infringement of certain patent rights and claiming royalties and punitive damages. The Company has filed a counter action, and preliminary hearings and discovery proceedings on both actions are in progress. Company officers and counsel believe the Company has a good chance of prevailing, but the ultimate outcome of the lawsuits cannot presently be determined. No provision for any liability that may result has been made in the financial statements, nor do the financial statements contain any disclosure of this matter.

In our opinion, except for the failure to disclose the pending lawsuit in the 19X5 financial statements as discussed in the preceding paragraph, the financial statements referred to above present fairly the consolidated financial position of J Company as of December 31, 19X5 and 19X4 and the consolidated results of its operations and the changes in its financial position for the years then ended, in conformity with generally accepted accounting principles applied on a consistent basis.

5. *Subject to* qualified opinion:

We have examined the consolidated balance sheets of J Company as of December 31, 19X5 and 19X4 and the statements of consolidated income, retained earnings, and changes in financial position for the years then ended. Our examinations were made in accordance with generally accepted auditing standards and, accordingly, included such tests of the accounting records and such other auditing procedures as we considered necessary in the circumstances.

During the current year the Company became a defendant in a lawsuit alleging infringement of certain patent rights and claiming royalties and punitive damages. The Company has filed a counter action, and preliminary hearings and discovery proceedings on both actions are in progress. Company officers and counsel believe the Company has a good chance of prevailing, but the ultimate outcome of the lawsuits cannot presently be determined. No provision for any liability that may result has been made in the financial statements, nor do the financial statements contain any disclosure of this matter.

In our opinion, subject to the effects, if any, on the 19X5 financial statements of the ultimate resolution of the matter discussed in the preceding paragraph, the financial statements referred to above present fairly the consolidated financial position of J Company as of

December 31, 19X5 and 19X4 and the consolidated results of its operations and the changes in its financial position for the years then ended, in conformity with generally accepted accounting principles applied on a consistent basis.

6. Adverse opinion:

We have examined the consolidated balance sheets of J Company as of December 31, 19X5 and 19X4 and the statements of consolidated income, retained earnings, and changes in financial position for the years then ended. Our examinations were made in accordance with generally accepted auditing standards and, accordingly, included such tests of the accounting records and such other auditing procedures as we considered necessary in the circumstances.

During the current year the Company became a defendant in a lawsuit alleging infringement of certain patent rights and claiming royalties and punitive damages. The Company has filed a counter action, and preliminary hearings and discovery proceedings on both actions are in progress. Company officers and counsel believe the Company has a good chance of prevailing, but the ultimate outcome of the lawsuits cannot presently be determined. No provision for any liability that may result has been made in the financial statements, nor do the financial statements contain any disclosure of this matter.

In our opinion, the 19X4 financial statements present fairly the consolidated financial position of J Company as of December 31, 19X4 and the consolidated results of its operations and the changes in its financial position for the year then ended, in conformity with generally accepted accounting principles applied on a consistent basis.

Further, in our opinion, because of the failure to disclose the lawsuit referred to above, the 19X5 financial statements do not present fairly, in conformity with generally accepted accounting principles, the consolidated financial position of J Company as of December 31, 19X5 or the consolidated results of its operations and changes in its financial position for the year then ended.

7. Disclaimer of opinion:

We have examined the consolidated balance sheets of J Company as of December 31, 19X5 and 19X4 and the statements of consolidated income, retained earnings, and changes in financial position for the years then ended. Our examinations were made in accordance with generally accepted auditing standards and, accordingly, included such tests of the accounting records and such other auditing procedures as we considered necessary in the circumstances.

During the current year the Company became a defendant in a lawsuit alleging infringement of certain patent rights and claiming royalties and punitive damages. The Company has filed a counter action, and preliminary hearings and discovery proceedings on both actions are in progress. Company officers and counsel believe the Company has a good chance of prevailing, but the ultimate outcome of the lawsuits cannot presently be determined. No provision for any liability that may result has been made in the financial statements, nor do the financial statements contain any disclosure of this matter.

In our opinion, the 19X4 financial statements present fairly the consolidated financial position of J Company as of December 31, 19X4 and the consolidated results of its operations and the changes in its financial position for the year then ended, in conformity with generally accepted accounting principles applied on a consistent basis.

Because of the uncertainty associated with the lawsuit referred to above, we are not able to express, and we do not express, an opinion on the 19X5 financial statements.

Opinion wording followed as closely as possible that given in Statement on Auditing Standards (SAS) Number 2 (AICPA 1974). To compare the effects of the different nonstandard opinion forms, it was necessary to conceive a set of circumstances that would, at least arguably, justify each of the five opinion forms, 3-7. There are probably no such circumstances. The facts given in the opinion middle paragraph could, however, conceivably justify each of the several opinions:

Opinion 3 would be justified if the auditor considered the facts to be important enough to deserve emphasis but felt that their effects would not be material.

Opinions 4 or 6 could be justified, depending on the auditor's assessment of materiality, on the basis of inadequate disclosure by the client. According to SAS Number 2, paragraph 17, "if the client declines to disclose essential data in a financial statement, the auditor should provide it in his report if practicable and should express a qualified or adverse opinion because the information has been omitted from the financial statements." (AICPA 1974)

Opinions 5 or 7 could be justified by paragraph 24 of SAS Number 2, again depending on one's assessment of materiality, on the basis of uncertainty about the outcome of the litigation and its effects. (AICPA 1974)

Some might argue that the use of opinion 4 or 6 in this case also requires either 5 or 7, and vice versa. Others would argue that the opinion wording given above is not only sufficient but preferable to complicating the opinion further to the probable confusion of the reader. These opinion forms were reviewed with several audit partners in CPA firms, and they concurred in the wording given. While every effort was made to develop opinion forms that would reflect actual practice, the acceptability of the wording in terms of professional standards was not the primary concern; the real issue was whether investors would view these opinion forms as realistic. On the basis of the judgments of the audit partners consulted and the absence of any investor feedback to the contrary, it appears that investors completely accepted the legitimacy of the audit opinions used.

The audit opinion was placed after the financial statements. According to a study by Purdy, Smith, and Gray (1969), this placement increases the likelihood of retention by the reader of the auditor's message.

The financial statement packet was accompanied by a response form that contained detailed instructions for each experimental task or response. Response forms were identified with audit-opinion type by an unobtrusive check mark varied as to location.

The experimental packet was reviewed with a number of academicians and practitioners in the fields of accounting and finance. Numerous revisions were made on the basis of these reviews and of pretesting.

Each opinion form constitutes one experimental treatment or X in the posttest-only-control-group experimental design described at the beginning of this chapter. In the regression analysis used to test hypotheses, the opinion form constituted an additional independent or control variable (coded as a dummy variable).

It should be noted that some opinion forms were not investigated in this study; these include the consistency exception, a qualification for scope limitation, and a going concern qualification (doubt exists about the ability of the company to continue as a going concern). Of course, qualified and adverse opinions and disclaimers could be rendered for many reasons other than those given. Other opinion forms might have different effects on investor behavior.

The complete experimental packet is reproduced in appendix A.

Hypotheses

The seven dependent variables and five audit-report forms result in thirty-five testable hypotheses. These can be summarized in two general versions corresponding to those presented at the end of chapter 3, restated here in the null form:

$H_O - 1$ The addition of a standard audit report to a set of financial statements will have no significant effect on (one of the seven dependent variables).

H_O-2 Replacement of a standard audit report with (one of four nonstandard audit reports) will have no significant effect on (one of the
seven dependent variables).

Subject Selection

Financial statements are used by many types of people—investors, bankers,
present and potential employees, government administrators, legislators,
social activists, and journalists. This study focuses only on investors. Even
so, investors will vary from those who are very knowledgeable about financial reporting to those who know practically nothing of it and rely entirely
on the advice of others, such as their brokers. Some will be very active while
others will leave their portfolios unchanged for years. Some will be wealthy,
others not.

It has been suggested that financial statements and audit reports should
be prepared for the reasonably sophisticated user, with little or no concern
for those who have no background or understanding of the complex rules
and standards governing financial reporting. For example, the Accounting
Principles Board declared, "Appropriate use of financial accounting information requires a knowledge of the characteristics and limitations of financial accounting" and "financial statement users are presumed to be generally familiar with business practices, the technical language of accounting,
and the nature of the information reported." (AICPA 1970) Others,
however, argue that financial statements and auditors' reports should serve
all users regardless of their level of sophistication.

Rather than choose sides in this argument, the experiment was designed
to provide evidence on the effect of auditors' reports on virtually all types
of investors. While the independent variables discussed previously allow for
control of a number of investor characteristics, it was necessary to draw
samples of subjects from several strata to insure adequate representation of
the full range of investor experience and knowledgeability. Samples were
therefore selected from three broad groups: professional investors,
shareholders, and general business-persons.

To reach professional investors and shareholders, lists of investment
money managers (institutional investors), security analysts with stockbrokers, and shareholders were purchased from Dunhill International List
Company. Dunhill confirmed that names were selected from alphabetical
lists using systematic random sampling. A review of lists for geographical
distribution indicated that the names selected were distributed among the
states in rough proportion to the concentrations expected among the three
populations.

The Dunhill shareholder lists may be biased in favor of males. Apparently their experience has indicated that the majority of stock held by females is for tax purposes, with the actual manipulation of the holdings done by males; consequently they eliminate a majority of the female names from their lists (Barnett 1976, p. 81).

General business-persons were accessed through classes in the College of Business Administration at Wichita State University. A cross section of classes were selected to obtain subjects with a broad range of personal characteristics, but with concentration on upper division and evening graduate courses. Wichita State University (WSU) is an urban university with a full range of day and evening classes. Because the average age of WSU students is considerably above the national norm and most of the business graduate students are employed full time, it was expected that these classes would provide a good cross-section of Wichita-area business-persons with a reasonably broad range of business and investment experience. As the personal characteristics reported in appendix C indicate, this expectation was realized.

The objective in using WSU classes was not to use students as surrogates for business-persons, but rather to obtain access to a cross section of business persons in a setting that would permit execution of the experiment. (This may not be a very important distinction. Ashton and Kramer's (1980) review of research on the use of students as surrogates indicated that students may be good surrogates for experiments involving decision making, but not for studies of attitudes and attitude changes.) Since a large overall sample size was obtained, it was only necessary to select samples so as to insure that reasonable numbers of subjects from various experience and personal categories were included. Finer representation was not necessary since the multiple-regression analysis used controls explicitly for differences in subject characteristics.

Administration of the Experiment

The professional investors and shareholders were randomly assigned to the two control and five test groups, and were mailed a preliminary postcard advising that they would soon be receiving important research material and requesting their participation. This was followed in a few days by the experimental packet (appendix A) with an accompanying cover letter, and by another postcard eight days after the primary mailing requesting those who had not already done so to complete and return the response form. These mailings were made during the summer of 1979.

For the Wichita State University classes, professors were contacted in advance to secure cooperation. Experimental materials along with detailed written instructions were provided to professors for the first class meeting of the spring 1978, semester. They were directed to distribute the packets in the prearranged sequence (packets were arranged in sequences of seven to achieve random assignment of subjects to groups), to identify the project as "a study of financial evaluation and decision making," and to advise students to complete a response form only if they had not already participated in another class. Debriefing of professors indicated no problems in administration. Numbers of experimental packets distributed and returned are indicated in table 4-1.

Estimates based on research data must be unbiased, free from systematic error. When data are obtained by sampling there are two broad sources of possible bias: nonresponse bias and response bias.

Nonresponse Bias

Nonresponse bias occurs when people participating in an experiment or responding to a survey differ systematically, on one or more measures of interest, from people not responding. Nonresponse bias is always a concern when participation or response is voluntary.

Prior research indicates that either a preliminary or a follow-up mailing should increase the rate of response in a study conducted by mail. For this study both preliminary and follow-up mailings were used. The low response rates obtained were probably due to the complexity of the experiment and oversampling of the groups by other researchers; as noted by Dyckman, Gibbins, and Swieringa (1975, p. 80), "The conduct of many studies in this area has left the typical respondents (e.g., financial analysts) less than enthusiastic about further participation." Although the absolute numbers of responses obtained are more than adequate for the statistical analyses used, the low response rates require special attention to the possibility of nonresponse bias.

Table 4-1
Experimental Packets Distributed and Returned

Population Sampled	Packets Distributed	Responses Received	Response Rate
Professional investors			
Institutional investors	1,500	224	15%
Security analysts	1,500	179	12
Shareholders	3,500	405	12
General business persons (WSU)	551	551	100
Totals	7,051	1,359	

Two methods are often suggested to test for nonresponse bias (see, for example, Oppenheim 1966; Dyckman, Gibbins, and Swieringa 1978; Buzby 1974):

1. Personal characteristics of the respondents may be compared to known or estimated characteristics of the population. Since research seeks data that are not already known, these comparisons must usually be made on characteristics other than those that are the subject of the research.
2. Early and late responses may be compared. Oppenheim (1966, p. 34) observes, "it has been found that respondents who send in their questionnaire very late are roughly similar to nonrespondents." If later responses differ significantly from earlier ones, the nonrespondents may similarly differ from those who responded and nonresponse bias may be present. On the other hand, if no significant difference is found between early and late responses on a variable of interest, we may have a reasonable basis for believing that respondents are similar to nonrespondents and are representative of the entire population.

Personal Characteristics. Personal characteristics of shareholders reported in the present study are compared in table 4-2 with data from (1) the New York Stock Exchange's (NYSE) 1975 interviews with a sample of 1,500 shareholders; (2) interviews with 404 shareholders conducted in 1974 by Opinion Research Corporation for Arthur Andersen & Co.; (3) Chang and Most's mail survey of U.S. shareholders (554 usable responses); and (4) Epstein's mail survey of round-lot shareholders (432 responses).

Nonresponse bias should be minimal or nonexistent in the NYSE and Arthur Andersen & Co. studies because interviews were used to collect data. The other three studies, including the present study, relied on mail responses. Shareholders responding in these studies appear to be better educated and to have larger investments in stocks than the population of shareholders. The participants in the present study are also predominantly male because, as noted earlier, the list-service company that was used purges most of the female names on the grounds that their experience indicates that spouse names are often used for tax purposes but the actual investment decisions are made primarily by males.

The other possible comparisons in table 4-2 provide inconclusive results. Age of shareholders in the present study is consistent with data reported by the NYSE, Chang and Most, and Epstein, but not with the Arthur Andersen results. A majority of the shareholders in the present study had some training in accounting or finance; this was also true of those responding to Chang and Most, but not for Epstein's respondents.

Thus it appears that shareholder participants in the present study differ from the population of shareholders by having more education, being

Table 4-2
Comparisons of Shareholder Personal Characteristics
(Percentage)

Characteristic	Present Study: Mail	NYSE (1975): Interviews	AA&Co. (1974): Interviews	Chang and Most (1979): Mail	Epstein (1975): Mail
Education					
No college	13	35	36	5	10
1–3 years college	13	23	23	14	17
4 or more years college	74	42	41	81	73
Value of stocks owned					
Under $10,000	14	50	n/a[a]	15	9
$10,000–$49,999	27	35	n/a	24	35
$50,000 and over	59	15	n/a	61	56
Age[b]					
Under 30	5	n/a	22	n/a	6
30–49	35	n/a	39	n/a	41
50 and over	60	n/a	39	n/a	53
44 and under	28	34	n/a	14	n/a
45–64	52	43	n/a	65	n/a
65 and over	20	23	n/a	21	n/a
Sex					
Male	94	50	55	n/a	n/a
Female	6	50	45	n/a	n/a
Training in accounting or finance					
Yes	59	n/a	n/a	64	36
No	41	n/a	n/a	36	64

[a]Data not provided
[b]Comparable categories were not used in all studies

predominantly male, and having larger investments in stocks. Comparable data for security analysts and institutional investors—the other groups sampled by mail—could not be found. It is probably reasonable to assume, however, that participants from these groups differ from their respective populations in the same manner.

We have determined that shareholders in this study differ from the population of shareholders on three characteristics. Are these characteristics significantly related to investment decisions and attitudes? A multiple-regression analysis was performed (see appendix D for an evaluation of assumptions necessary for multiple regression) to investigate the effects of these three characteristics on the seven dependent variables for all the mail participants in the study (not only shareholders). Significant effects were discovered (alpha = .05) in the following cases:

> Shareholders with more years of college, as well as those with larger investments in common stock, were less inclined to agree that the J Company is successful and that its management is well qualified.

> Men were more willing to invest in the J Company than were women. This result may be unreliable because of the small proportion—about 5 percent—of women who participated by mail in the study. (Even if the result is reliable, no conclusion can be drawn from it regarding the relative investment conservatism or risk propensity of men versus women shareholders, since that portion of the $100,000 not invested in the J Company was also required to be invested immediately, in other NYSE-listed companies.)

Early versus Late Responses. The date of receipt was recorded on each response; number of days elapsed from the date of the original mailing were then calculated and coded for computer analysis. A multiple-regression analysis was made using days elapsed as the dependent variable while controlling simultaneously for both the set of fourteen control variables and the set of seven dependent variables listed earlier in this chapter (whether a variable is a dependent or a control variable depends, of course, on the specific analysis being performed). No significant relationship was found between the total set of twenty-one variables and the number of days elapsed before responding.

A second multiple-regression analysis was performed to determine whether number of days elapsed in responding is significantly related to any of the seven decision and attitude responses. No significant relationships were found (alpha = .05), indicating that these responses do not differ systematically between early and later respondents.

The earliest 10 percent of responses and the last 10 percent were then identified and a series of *t*-tests were performed to determine whether later respondents differed in any significant respects from the earlier ones. Later respondents were found to:

have significantly less business experience;

have significantly less college credit in finance and investment courses;

have significantly smaller investments in stocks, bonds, and other securities;

evaluate stocks or advise other investors significantly less frequently;

estimate a significantly higher price for J Company stock.

These results are consistent with those obtained in the personal-characteristics comparisons, and are also consistent with the results of other research (see Armstrong and Overton 1977, for discussion and references).

Of the significant differences found, only one—the higher J Company stock-price estimate by later respondents—involves a decision or attitude response (a behavioral response) as opposed to a personal characteristic. A question is therefore raised as to whether the responses on this estimate are representative of the population. We cannot, however, determine from these data whether different audit opinions would produce different stock price estimates between respondents and nonrespondents. The data raise a question but produce no answer.

Finally, analysis was performed to determine whether a systematic relationship exists between the four groups studied and the opinion forms. In other words, were the seven audit-opinion versions distributed evenly, or was there a concentration of one or another version? (Note that the final distribution of opinion forms among those responding by mail could vary from the distribution of forms mailed if all were not returned.) In a perfectly even distribution, each version would appear in 1/7 or 14.29 percent of the responses. Actual proportions ranged from 11.1 percent to 18.8 percent. The lambda statistic, a measure of association for SPSS crosstabulations based on nominal-level variables (Nie et al. 1973, p. 225) was computed at .006. Since lambda can range from a value of .0, indicating no association whatsoever, to 1.0, indicating perfect association, it appears that no association exists between investor group and opinion versions and that the distribution of opinion forms in the responses returned is satisfactorily even or rectangular.

Nonresponse-Bias Summary. As can be expected in a study that relies partially on mail responses, some nonresponse bias appears to be present in the data. Compared to the population of investors, respondents in this study may be somewhat more negative about the J Company and its management, and may estimate a lower price for J Company stock. Whether respondents and nonrespondents would react differently to different audit opinion forms can only be hypothesized. In terms of the identifiable effects on responses, it appears that nonresponse bias does not present a serious barrier to generalization of the results of this study to the investment and business community.

Response Bias

Response bias may be defined as a difference between the true value for a variable and that reported by a respondent. There are several possible causes of response bias.

1. *Are subjects able to answer correctly*? This possible source of response bias is of concern primarily with questions calling for factual responses, and is therefore not an issue for the dependent variables in this study, which call for attitudinal assessments, estimates, and projections. Among the control variables, those that could have caused some difficulty include years of business experience, market value of investments, and number of stock transactions within the past two years. Lack of knowledge would most likely result in no response; nonresponse is a different problem and does not of itself produce response bias. The number of blank responses in these three areas (three questions related to market value of different types of investments are combined as one for this discussion) were 23 (1.7 percent), 57 (4.2 percent), and 39 (2.9 percent) respectively. Missing values for other factual-type questions ranged from 3 (sex) to 53 (credit hours in accounting courses). It was not practical to attempt to independently ascertain the true values on these three characteristics for the persons who participated in this study. Nevertheless, in the light of the relatively large numbers of blank or missing responses, we can probably assume that some difficulty was encountered by several respondents in answering these three questions and that, consequently, the answers that were given may, in some cases, be inaccurate and contain a limited but unmeasurable amount of response bias.

2. *Are subjects willing to answer correctly, or will their answers be exaggerated or outright false*? This source of bias is most likely to occur when subjects are liable to seek a particular effect from their answers, such as impressing the researcher or avoiding embarrassment. There would appear to be little danger from such bias in this study since respondent anonymity was assured and maintained. Further, the study involved mainly professional people who, we can hope, are not given to automatic and habitual lying when nothing is at stake.

A related problem can occur when subjects do not take an experiment seriously and provide responses that would not be consistent with their actual behavior in similar "real world" situations. This problem is present in every experiment, and is the major disadvantage of experimental research that offsets, or is offset by, the advantage of maintaining experimental control over a number of factors to focus on the one variable of interest. In this study instructions were designed to evoke a serious response; pretesting and evaluation indicate that this objective was achieved. Based on the pretest experience and the internal consistency of responses, it appears that those who participated did so seriously, while those who were not willing to give the experiment serious attention simply did not respond.

3. *Do subjects understand the questions*? Misunderstanding can, of course, produce wrong answers. For this study the experimental materials and response form went through several cycles of testing and revision to identify and eliminate possible sources of misunderstanding. Instructions were expanded and, where appropriate, responses were illustrated. A careful review of each response indicates that these efforts were successful, with three possible exceptions. A small number of respondents apparently misinterpreted the questions about credit hours in accounting and finance, and responded with the number of continuing-education/professional-development class-hours experienced. A few professional investors evidently reported the market value of investments managed or held by their firms, instead of reporting personal investments. And the income projections for J Company made by a limited number of subjects reflected a misunderstanding either of the question or of accounting and the meaning of income (some were clearly sales projections; others were obviously projections of the retained-earnings balance). In all three cases, extreme and unrealistic responses were treated as missing values. While this interpretation and treatment may, of course, have been in error, it is a less dangerous error than permitting what are essentially "garbage" values to enter the analysis.

4. *Are responses recorded as intended*? When a subject intends to check "yes" and accidentally checks "no," response bias results. Such errors inevitably occur when a large number of different individuals are recording answers on an unfamiliar form. Two steps were taken to counter this problem: the response form was carefully pretested, evaluated, and revised several times to minimize the likelihood of recording error; and all responses were reviewed manually and through several computer analyses to identify inconsistent or unrealistic responses. Unless the correct meaning was clear in the context, such responses were treated as missing values.

It is almost impossible to totally eliminate response bias from a study that involves a large number of subjects, but great care was taken in this study to reduce response bias to a minimum. When a suspect answer is encountered, it can be accepted, adjusted to reflect the researcher's estimate of the correct answer or the answer that was intended, replaced by some sort of average, or treated as a blank response or missing value. Adjustment of responses is very risky, and was undertaken only when the intended answer was almost certain. Replacement by an average is sometimes advocated, especially as a way of maximizing the number of usable responses. Because of the large number of subjects in this experiment (1,359), the more conservative approach was used, and responses about which there was significant doubt were treated as missing values.

Bias from any source can distort research results. In this study, however, absolute bias in responses is less important (although still of concern) than relative bias. The primary objective of the study is to investigate the differential effects of several audit-opinion forms, compared to each other and to no opinion, on investor behavior and attitudes. Error or bias in measurement of the absolute value of a decision or attitude variable is thus less important than error in measurement of the *difference* in a response between control and test groups. Some sources of possible bias, being inherent in the experiment, instruments used, or setting, would have a consistent effect across all subjects, producing errors in absolute values, but little or no error in differences among groups. This characteristic of the present study by no means eliminates any concern over response and nonresponse bias, but fortunately does result in a reduced risk compared to a descriptive study that seeks to estimate the absolute value of some variable.

Review of Response Forms

Reponse forms were carefully desk-checked for obvious errors. Audit-opinion form, Dow Jones Industrial Average, and number of days elapsed until return of form were encoded based on prior coded markings on the response form, the date recorded by the subject, and date of response-form receipt, respectively. Response data were then key-punched and verified, and several editing computer runs were made to check for inconsistent or unrealistic data.

Statistical Analysis

The research was designed to control for variations in personal characteristics of respondents statistically, as well as through random selection and assignment. Based on a review of prior research and independent analysis, several personal characteristics and exogenous variables were identified that might have a significant effect on behavior; along with a dummy variable denoting the audit-opinion form, these become the independent variables in a multivariate analysis. The effect of such an analysis is to account for the change in the dependent variable associated with a difference in audit opinions (a change in the dummy variable of one unit) while holding all other variables constant. It is as if we were able to construct two paired samples, with the members of each pair exactly alike as to age, years of business experience, investing experience, portfolio size, and so forth, but receiving different audit-opinion forms (or one receiving a standard opinion and the other receiving no opinion). Any difference in response is then attributable to the difference in audit-opinion form plus an error term representing the aggregate effect of any unidentified variables.

Given a combination of dichotomous (nonmetric) and quantitative (metric) variables, analysis of covariance is the indicated form of multivariate analysis. Although analysis of covariance may be performed using either analysis of variance or multiple-regression routines, multiple regression was selected for several reasons:

1. Analysis of variance requires predictors that are independent, and this is often interpreted to require equal numbers of cases in the cells. Equal cell sizes can be obtained when subjects are assigned to cells (for example, five subjects are chosen in each age category), but are not feasible in an experiment with subjects selected from a large population by mail.
2. The analysis of variance procedure available in the Statistical Package for the Social Sciences (Nie et al. 1975) allows a maximum of five factors (nonmetric variables) and five covariates (metric variables). In this study it was necessary to evaluate more than five metric variables.
3. In addition to allowing tests of hypotheses, multiple regression produces beta coefficients that serve as estimates of the amount of change in the dependent variable associated with the different audit opinions, controlling for all other independent variables. To be precise, the beta, or partial-regression coefficient, "indicates the expected *difference* on Y between two groups that happen to differ on X_1 by one unit but equal on X_2," and all other X_i (Nie et al. 1975, p. 330). Thus if we find, for example, that an adverse opinion significantly reduces the amount an investor would be willing to invest in the J Company, the beta will provide a point estimate of this reduction (and also enable us to calculate a confidence interval for the reduction).

Multiple regression relies on several assumptions. An extensive discussion and evaluation of these assumptions is presented in appendix D.

As discussed earlier in this chapter, prior research studies were reviewed to identify eleven personal characteristics and other factors that might have a significant effect on investor behavior and attitudes; to these were added three variables original with this study. It was, of course, not possible to know in advance which of these fourteen variables would figure significantly in the behavior of investors in this study. Tests were therefore made to identify those variables that appear to contribute significantly to explanation of investor behavior, and to determine whether significant multicollinearity exists among the independent variables.

Although extreme multicollinearity was not present, some was identified among three sets of variables; a factor analysis also indicated that each of these three sets constitutes a factor. Consequently three interactive variables were created as follows:

YEARSX = Square root of (years of business experience × age)

HOURSX = Square root of (accounting hours × finance hours)

TOTAL INVESTMENTS = Market value of stocks + market value of bonds + market value of other securities

These additions resulted in seventeen possible control variables, besides the dummy variable representing the audit-opinion form. Although we would like to control for as many behavior determinants, besides the audit-opinion form, as possible, inclusion of irrelevant independent variables is not cost-free; there can be three unfortunate consequences (Wonnacott and Wonnacott 1970, p. 312):

1. Any test on betas for relevant variables will be weakened by inclusion of betas for irrelevant variables, for the following two reasons.
2. There will be fewer degrees of freedom in the residuals to estimate σ^2.
3. The estimator for each of the relevant betas will be more variable than it would be under the proper specification.

Since the statistic of primary interest in this study is the beta for the dummy variable representing the audit opinion form, and since this will be less reliable if irrelevant variables are included in the model, model specification becomes quite important.

Three criteria were considered for inclusion of control variables in the regression equations (this search procedure is sometimes referred to as Fritsch's method):

1. The variable is consistent with the conceptual model.
2. The variable exhibits a significant coefficient sign which is consistent with a priori expectations or previous research results.
3. Inclusion of the variable serves to increase the corrected coefficient of determination.

Based on these criteria and the evaluation of multiple-regression assumptions (appendix D), a set of control variables was selected for each of the equations used to test the hypotheses listed at the end of chapter 3. These equations, and the results of the tests of hypotheses, are discussed in chapter 5.

5 Results of the Experiments

This chapter presents the results of the experiments to investigate the effects of audit reports on investor behavior. Each of the seven behavioral responses is discussed, followed by a summary of the effects of each of the five opinion forms.

An estimating equation was derived for each behavioral response, or dependent variable Y, from the combined set of 1,359 cases. These equations reflect the results of, and modifications made in response to, tests for linearity, interaction, and significance. Higher-order variables were added when they significantly increased the multiple coefficient of determination (R^2). Interactive variables were created by multiplying two variables together and taking the square root of the result, when such variables contributed significantly to the multiple R^2. A variable was dropped from an equation when its partial F statistic, which assesses the additional contribution of that variable to the prediction of Y over and above what is contributed by the other variables in the equation, was not significant at an alpha of .10 or less (that is, when the probability exceeded .10 that a partial-regression coefficient, or beta, as large as that associated with the independent variable under consideration could be obtained by chance.)

The beta coefficients in the estimating equations will differ depending on the audit-report form being evaluated. For this reason, the coefficients for the control variables will be reported only for the most frequently encountered form of audit report, the standard, unqualified opinion.

Income Projection

Subjects were asked to project the hypothetical J Company's net income for the following year, after examining comparative financial statements and a five-year statistical summary for the company. Responses are in thousands of dollars. This variable is used as a surrogate for the subject's assessment of the future outlook for the company.

Net income after taxes was reported as growing from $7,833,000 to $11,252,000 over the past five-year period, a 9.5 percent annual compounded-growth-rate. A linear projection at this rate would have produced an estimate for the next year of $12,321,000.

The estimating equation for income projection, based on the responses of the subjects who received financial statements accompanied by a standard, unqualified audit report, is:

$$\text{INCOME PROJECTION} = + 27822.640$$
$$+ \quad 287.017 \text{ (STOCK EVALUATIONS)}$$
$$- \quad 18.002 \text{ (ACTUAL DJIA)}$$
$$- \quad 480.284 \text{ (INVESTMENT ATTITUDE)}$$

$$\text{Multiple } R = 0.19169$$
$$R^2 = 0.03675$$
$$F = 2.00 \text{ with 3 and 157 degrees of freedom}$$

This model indicates that 3 to 4 percent of the variation in an investor's projection of income can be accounted for by recent experience in evaluating stocks, current attitude about investing in common stocks, and the influence of the current state of the market as reflected in the Dow Jones Industrial Average.

Standard Audit-Report

To evaluate the effect of the standard audit report compared to no audit report, a dummy variable for AUDIT OPINION was added. This variable is assigned a value of 1.0 for cases (subjects) when the financial statements are accompanied by a standard opinion, and a value of 0.0 when no opinion at all accompanies the statements. Applying the model to these cases produced the statistics in table 5-1 for the standard audit opinion. The beta value, or partial-regression coefficient, suggests that the presence of a standard or "clean" audit-opinion results in an increase of $546,838 in the estimate of income (note that income projections are expressed in thousands of dollars), from $12,054,220 to $12,601,058; this is a change of 4.5 percent. The F value for the audit opinion is significant at an alpha of .10 but not at .05.

Table 5-1
Test Statistics: Effect of Standard Audit Report on Income Projection

Beta	+ 546.838
Standard error of beta	313.130
F	3.05
Degrees of freedom	1 and 327

Nonstandard Audit Reports

The effects on income projection of four nonstandard audit-report forms were also tested—the *except for* opinion qualified for noncompliance with generally accepted accounting principles, the *subject to* opinion qualified because of uncertainty about the outcome of a future event, the adverse opinion, which says that the financial statements are not fairly presented, and the disclaimer due to extreme uncertainty about the outcome of a future event. The differential effects of these report forms could not be determined by comparing them with statements unaccompanied by an audit opinion, since each such opinion also provides additional information in a middle paragraph that could influence behavior. Instead, an opinion form for the control group was developed that included the first and last paragraphs of a standard opinion plus an additional middle paragraph providing an explanation of a contingency that was not disclosed by the reporting company. Since each nonstandard report also included this middle paragraph, the four test groups could then be compared to the control group to identify the differential effect of each nonstandard report form compared to the standard report form, while holding information about the contingency constant.

Four separate analyses were performed for the four nonstandard report forms. Subjects receiving the standard opinion with the middle paragraph (the control group) and those receiving the *except for* opinion (the test group) provided the data for the first analysis: those receiving the standard opinion with a middle paragraph and those receiving the *subject to* opinion provided data for the second analysis, and so on.

Statistics for tests on the four nonstandard report forms are given in table 5-2. None of the *F* ratios is significant, so we cannot conclude that any of the four nonstandard report forms has a differential effect on investors' projections of a company's net income.

Table 5-2
Test Statistics: Effect of Nonstandard Audit-Report Forms on Income Projection

	Except for Opinion	Subject to Opinion	Adverse Opinion	Disclaimer
Beta	− 197.392	+ 13.253	− 154.036	− 54.225
Standard error of beta	201.905	182.519	195.168	203.063
F	0.96	0.01	0.62	0.07
Degrees of freedom	1 and 329	1 and 347	1 and 329	1 and 347

Share-Price Estimate

When evaluating a stock, investors must decide whether it represents an attractive buy at the current price (or the price expected to prevail at the time a buy order is executed). Different approaches are taken in reaching this decision, including a general assessment that the current price is high or low. A commonly used systematic approach involves calculating a fair price (usually using a risk-adjusted price/earnings multiple, but often including other data), then comparing this with the current price. The current price for J Company was given as $12 per share in a section dealing with an investment (see appendix A); subjects were later asked to give their estimate of a fair price for J Company common stock.

The equation for the estimate of a fair price for J Company common stock is:

$$
\begin{aligned}
\text{SHARE PRICE ESTIMATE} = &+ 13.197 \\
&- 0.003 \ (\text{DJIA ESTIMATE ERROR}) \\
&- 0.031 \ (\text{AGE}) \\
&+ 0.447 \ (\text{INVESTMENT ATTITUDE})
\end{aligned}
$$

$$
\text{Multiple } R = 0.20075
$$
$$
R^2 = 0.04030
$$
$$
F = 2.31 \text{ with 3 and 165 degrees of freedom}
$$

Although the entire set of independent variables (see appendix B) was tested, only these three turned out to be significant, and they accounted for only 4 percent of the variation in share-price estimates.

Standard Audit Report

Statistics to test the differential effect of a standard audit opinion, compared to no opinion, on investors' estimates of a fair price for J Company's common stock are presented in table 5-3. The critical value of the F ratio is

Table 5-3
Test Statistics: Effect of Standard Audit Report on Share-Price Estimate

Beta	−0.95
Standard error of beta	0.59
F	2.60
Degrees of freedom	1 and 338

2.71 at a significance level of .10 (1.32 at a significance level of .25). It therefore appears that the indicated effect of the standard audit report just misses being significant at the .10 level, and the null hypothesis is not rejected. We do not conclude that the audit report significantly affects the share-price estimate.

Nonstandard Audit Reports

Statistics for testing the effects of the four nonstandard audit-report forms on investors' share-price estimates are given in table 5-4. The insignificant F ratios do not permit rejection of the null hypotheses, and the conclusion indicated is that the several nonstandard audit-report forms, compared to the standard form, do not have a significant effect on investors' assessments of share prices. This conclusion suggests that company executives need not be overly concerned about the effect of a qualified, or even adverse, audit opinion on the price of their common stock.

Company Evaluation

Subjects were asked to indicate their agreement or disagreement with the statement, "J Company is a successful company," by placing a mark in one of five positions on a five-position scale with only the polar positions labeled (see appendix A). Responses were coded 0 to 4, with 0 denoting "strongly disagree" and 4 meaning "strongly agree." Thus positive coefficients in the estimating equation indicate an increase in agreement, and vice versa. The equation derived from subjects' responses is

Table 5-4
Test Statistics: Effect of Nonstandard Audit-Report Forms on Share-Price Estimate

	Except for Opinion	Subject to Opinion	Adverse Opinion	Disclaimer
Beta	−0.09	−0.32	−0.50	−0.22
Standard error of beta	0.53	0.45	0.58	0.56
F	0.03	0.51	0.72	0.15
Degrees of freedom	1 and 318	1 and 339	1 and 339	1 and 354

COMPANY EVALUATION = + 2.164
+ 0.052 (YEARS OF COLLEGE)
+ 0.033 (STOCK TRANSACTIONS)
− 0.138 (STOCK EVALUATIONS)
+ 0.005 (AGE)
+ 0.541 (INVESTMENT ATTITUDE)
− 0.140 (INVESTMENT ATTITUDE)^2
− 0.057 (STOCKHOLDER
dummy variable)
− 0.836 (SECURITY ANALYST
dummy variable)
− 0.544 (INSTITUTIONAL INVESTOR
dummy variable)

Multiple R = 0.37510
R^2 = 0.14070
F = 3.02 with 9 and 166 degrees of freedom

Each of the three dummy variables in this equation assumes the value 1.0 or 0.0 depending on the type of subject. (Thus, if the subject is from the other-business-persons category, all three dummy variables will be 0.0; if the subject is a stockholder, the STOCKHOLDER variable will be 1.0 and the other two will be 0.0; and so on.)

The model accounts for 14 percent of the variation in subjects' overall evaluation of the company.

Standard Audit Report

Addition of a standard audit report to J Company's financial statement does not significantly affect investors' evaluation of the company, as indicated in table 5-5.

Table 5-5
Test Statistics: Effect of Standard Audit Report on Company Evaluation

Beta	+0.039
Standard error of beta	0.115
F	0.12
Degrees of freedom	1 and 347

Nonstandard Audit Reports

As shown in table 5-6, only the adverse opinion has a clearly significant effect on investors' overall evaluation of the company; the F ratio for the adverse opinion is significant at the .05 level, while the F ratio for the *except for* opinion just misses being significant at the .10 level. On the scale of 0 (strongly disagree) to 4 (strongly agree), these results indicate that an adverse audit opinion would decrease the company evaluation from a scale value of 2.68 to one of 2.47.

Management Evaluation

In an attempt to isolate any report form effect on investors' evaluation of management, subjects were asked to indicate agreement or disagreement with the statement, "It appears that the management of J Company is well qualified." As with the company evaluation response, a five-position scale was used and answers were coded from 0, strongly disagree, to 4, strongly agree. The multiple-regression analysis resulted in the following model:

MANAGEMENT
EVALUATION = + 2.266
− 0.019 (YEARS OF COLLEGE)
− 0.135 (STOCK EVALUATIONS)
+ 0.011 (AGE)
+ 0.489 (INVESTMENT ATTITUDE)
− 0.116 (INVESTMENT ATTITUDE)^2
− 0.129 (STOCKHOLDER
dummy variable)
− 0.597 (SECURITY ANALYST
dummy variable)
− 0.566 (INSTITUTIONAL INVESTOR
dummy variable)
− 0.006 (TOTAL CREDITS)

Multiple R = 0.40993
R^2 = 0.16804
F = 3.70 with 9 and 165 degrees of freedom

Some improvement is seen in the explanatory power of this model compared to that for the company evaluation, with 17 percent of the total variation in management evaluation explained by the equation.

Table 5-6
Test Statistics: Effect of Nonstandard Audit-Report Forms
on Company Evaluation

	Except for Opinion	Subject to Opinion	Adverse Opinion	Disclaimer
Beta	−0.166	−0.056	−0.204	−0.055
Standard error of beta	0.103	0.103	0.100	0.101
F	2.61	0.30	4.19	0.30
Degrees of freedom	1 and 334	1 and 344	1 and 342	1 and 365

Standard Audit Report

The statistics in table 5-7 indicate that the presence of a standard audit opinion, when contrasted with financial statements accompanied by no audit report at all, produces no significant change in investors' evaluation of management's qualifications. Since the auditor's report says nothing directly about management, this result might have been expected.

Nonstandard Audit Reports

Table 5-8 reveals that two audit report forms, the *except for* opinion and the adverse opinion, reduce investors' evaluation of management to a degree that is significant at a probability below .10. The *except for* qualification reduces the scale value by 0.21, from 2.52 to 2.31; the adverse opinion causes a reduction of 0.19, from 2.51 to 2.32 (on a scale of 0 to 4). While the auditor's report does not speak to management's qualifications, these results indicate that management's reputation can be damaged by audit reports that are considered to be negative or critical.

Table 5-7
Test Statistics: Effect of Standard Audit Report on
Management Evaluation

Beta	−0.114
Standard error of beta	0.108
F	0.01
Degrees of freedom	1 and 343

Table 5-8
Test Statistics: Effect of Nonstandard Audit-Report Forms
on Management Evaluation

	Except for Opinion	Subject to Opinion	Adverse Opinion	Disclaimer
Beta	−0.208	−0.196	−0.190	−0.063
Standard error of beta	0.110	0.104	0.104	0.104
F	3.61	0.04	3.32	0.37
Degrees of freedom	1 and 334	1 and 342	1 and 353	1 and 364

Investment Decision

A scenario was presented in which the subjects were required to invest a sum of $100,000 in common stocks of companies listed on the New York Stock Exchange, and to indicate the portion of this amount they would choose to invest in the hypothetical J Company (see appendix A for details). Responses were given in dollar amounts ranging from $0 to $100,000. The estimating equation for this decision is

$$
\begin{aligned}
\text{INVESTMENT} = \ & -\ 270,415 \\
& +\quad 550\ \text{(YEARS OF COLLEGE)} \\
& -\quad 5,617\ \text{(STOCK EVALUATIONS)} \\
& +\quad 405\ \text{(ACTUAL DJIA)} \\
& +\quad 3,585\ \text{(INVESTMENT ATTITUDE)} \\
& -\quad 44,597\ \text{(STOCKHOLDER dummy variable)} \\
& -\quad 50,707\ \text{(SECURITY ANALYST dummy variable)} \\
& -\quad 47,433\ \text{(INSTITUTIONAL INVESTOR dummy variable)}
\end{aligned}
$$

$$
\begin{aligned}
\text{Multiple } R &= 0.52571 \\
R^2 &= 0.27638 \\
F &= 9.33 \text{ with 7 and 171 degrees of freedom}
\end{aligned}
$$

Four variables plus an indication of investor category account for about 28 percent of the variation in this particular investment decision. Of these, the most important variable is the actual Dow Jones Industrial Average at the time of the experiment; an increase of ten points in the Dow was associated with an increase of some $4,000 in the amount an investor would put into J Company common stock.

Standard Audit Report

Are investors likely to avoid a company that provides them only with unaudited financial statements? The *F* ratio in table 5-9 is not significant at any reasonable probability; thus the presence or absence of a standard audit opinion appears to make little difference to investors. They were as willing to invest in the J Company when no audit report at all was attached to the financial statements, as they were when a standard, unqualified report was attached. If the audit report adds credibility to financial statements, this is not translated into a differential investment decision.

Nonstandard Audit Reports

Statistics for the effect on the investment decision of nonstandard audit-report forms are given in table 5-10. By examining the *F* ratios we can see that neither the *except for* nor the *subject to* qualification significantly affects the investor's willingness to invest in the reporting company's common stock, while the effect of the disclaimer would be significant only at a fairly high level of probability (between .10 and .25). The adverse opinion has a significant negative effect, at the .10 significance level, on the amount investors are willing to put into the J Company; compared to the $29,661 average investment when a standard opinion (with explanatory middle paragraph) is present, the adverse opinion results in an investment of $24,491, a 17 percent reduction.

The tests on the investment decision lead to the conclusions that (1) investors pay little or no attention to whether a company's financial statements have been audited, and (2) when a nonstandard audit report is presented with the statements, only the adverse opinion will have a significant effect (and that will of course be negative) on the investment decision.

Confidence in the Investment Decision

Immediately following the investment decision, subjects were told to indicate their confidence in that decision on a scale of 0 to 10, with 0 signifying no confidence at all and 10 representing complete confidence. This variable was included to test the widely held view that an audit report adds credibility to and increases investor confidence in financial statements. If the investor has more confidence in the statements, we would expect this to be reflected in greater confidence in an investment decision based on those statements.

Of the seven behavioral responses studied, regression models for the other six included from three to seven significant independent variables (counting the investor-classification dummy variables as one). The confidence-rating equation requires nineteen, although only ten of these are based on raw responses; the remainder are transformations of original variables to control for interaction and curvilinear relationships. The confidence rating equation is

CONFIDENCE RATING =   − 11.60810
                          + 1.15702 (EXPERIENCE)
                          + 0.26014 × 10^{-2} (EXPERIENCE)^2
                          − 0.00155 (DJIA ESTIMATE ERROR)
                          + 1.78343 (STOCK EVALUATIONS)
                          − 0.27974 (STOCK EVALUATIONS)^2
                          − 0.38335 (SEX)
                          − 0.35813 (AGE)
                          + 0.60689 × 10^{-2} (AGE)^2
                          + 0.02543 (ACTUAL DJIA)
                          − 0.37723 × 10^{-5} (INVESTMENT
                                      DECISION)
                          + 0.32955 × 10^{-9} (INVESTMENT
                                      DECISION)^2
                          − 0.13626 × 10^{-14} (INVESTMENT
                                      DECISION)^3
                          + 0.73729 (INVESTMENT ATTITUDE)
                          − 0.64464 × 10^{-2} (INVESTMENT
                                      ATTITUDE)^2
                          − 1.65061 (STOCKHOLDER
                                      dummy variable)
                          − 0.69156 (SECURITY ANALYST
                                      dummy variable)
                          − 2.18467 (INSTITUTIONAL
                                      INVESTOR dummy
                                      variable)
                          − 0.44293 (YEARSX)
                          − 0.01414 (YEARSX)^2
                          + 0.15772 (TOTAL CREDITS)
                          − 0.24669 (HOURSX)

               Multiple R =   0.57322
                    R^2 =   0.32858
                      F =   3.40 with 21 and 146 degrees of freedom

(Extra decimal places are given because of the magnitude of the raw values of some of the independent variables.)

Unless the ratio of sample size to number of independent variables is quite large, say 100:1, the multiple correlation coefficient will be biased

Table 5-9
Test Statistics: Effect of Standard Audit Report on
Investment Decision

Beta	− 3,149
Standard error of beta	3,294
F	0.91
Degrees of freedom	1 and 353

upward. While this upward bias is insignificant for the other six estimating equations, it is more serious in this case with twenty-one independent variables. Based on a formula given by Nunnally (1978, p. 180), an unbiased estimate of R would be 0.48642, and for R^2, 0.23660.

This model indicates that investor confidence in an investment decision increases with business experience, experience in recent stock transactions, the level of the Dow Jones Industrial Average, a positive attitude about investing currently in common stocks, and the number of college credits in accounting and finance courses. Confidence decreases with lack of familiarity with the Dow Jones Industrial Average (and presumably with the stock market), gender (women are less confident than men), age (older persons are less confident), and the magnitude of the investment decision itself (larger investments are associated with lower confidence). In addition, stockholders, security analysts, and institutional investors—the more sophisticated investors—are less confident than the general business population (ignorance is bliss?); this is probably due to the desire of the sophisticated investor for more information about the company and about market and economic conditions than was provided in the experiment.

Standard Audit Report

According to the conventional wisdom (see chapter 3), the auditor's report adds credibility to and increases confidence in financial statements. If these effects actually do occur, they do not appear to be translated into increased confidence in decisions made on the basis of such statements. Table 5-11 shows that a standard audit report appended to financial statements produced no significant increase in confidence in the investment decision; the F ratio is not significant at any reasonable alpha level.

Nonstandard Audit Reports

As with the standard audit-report, so with the four nonstandard versions tested: they produce no significant change in confidence in the investment

Table 5-10
Test Statistics: Effect of Nonstandard Audit-Report Forms
on Investment Decision

	Except for Opinion	Subject to Opinion	Adverse Opinion	Disclaimer
Beta	− 1,714	+ 1,178	− 5,170	− 4,219
Standard error of beta	3,131	3,110	2,931	2,992
F	0.30	0.14	3.11	1.99
Degrees of freedom	1 and 347	1 and 364	1 and 359	1 and 375

decision (see table 5-12). Recall that the comparison in each case is to a standard opinion with an explanatory middle paragraph. The addition of the auditor's qualification to this paragraph, or even an adverse opinion or disclaimer, fails to significantly affect the investor's confidence in his or her investment decision. While numerous factors impact significantly on the confidence rating, the audit-report form is not one of them.

Assessment of Fraud

According to prior studies based on surveys and interviews, substantial numbers of investors and other business-persons believe an independent audit of financial statements provides assurance that fraud has not been committed. To test the effect of this belief in an experimental context, subjects were asked to indicate their agreement, on a scale of 0 to 4 (with 0 signifying strongly disagree and 4 meaning strongly agree) with the statement, "It appears that the risk of fraud in the J Company is low." (Several versions of this statement were pretested before this somewhat awkward wording was settled on as providing the most valid and reliable measure.) If an audit report really does provide assurance to investors that no fraud has been committed, the standard audit report should increase the mean scale value for this response.

Table 5-11
Test Statistics: Effect of Standard Audit Report on
Confidence Rating

Beta	+ 0.11
Standard error of beta	0.27
F	0.15
Degrees of freedom	1 and 334

The following estimating equation resulted from the multiple-regression analyses for this variable:

$$
\begin{aligned}
\text{ASSESSMENT OF FRAUD} = \ & +\ 10.132 \\
& -\ 0.020\ (\text{EXPERIENCE}) \\
& -\ 0.004\ (\text{YEARS OF COLLEGE}) \\
& +\ 0.003\ (\text{AGE}) \\
& -\ 0.010\ (\text{ACTUAL DJIA}) \\
& +\ 0.008\ (\text{INVESTMENT ATTITUDE}) \\
& +\ 0.215\ (\text{STOCKHOLDER dummy variable}) \\
& +\ 0.370\ (\text{SECURITY ANALYST dummy variable}) \\
& +\ 0.171\ (\text{INSTITUTIONAL INVESTOR dummy variable}) \\
& -\ 0.017\ (\text{TOTAL CREDITS})
\end{aligned}
$$

$$
\begin{aligned}
\text{Multiple } R &= 0.37739 \\
R^2 &= 0.14243 \\
F &= 3.40 \text{ with 9 and 165 degrees of freedom}
\end{aligned}
$$

This model indicates that older and more active investors (as opposed to business-persons generally), and those with a positive attitude about investing in common stocks, are less suspicious of fraud in a reporting company. Suspicion of fraud is increased with years of business experience, years of college, credits in accounting and finance courses, and any decline in the Dow Jones Industrial Average (as the market goes down suspicion of fraud goes up.)

Standard Audit Report

If the standard or clean version of the audit opinion provides reassurance that fraud has not occurred, this effect is not significant. Table 5-13 shows that

Table 5-12
Test Statistics: Effect of Nonstandard Audit-Report Forms on Confidence Rating

	Except for *Opinion*	Subject to *Opinion*	*Adverse Opinion*	*Disclaimer*
Beta	−0.14	+0.31	+0.18	+0.18
Standard error of beta	0.28	0.25	0.25	0.25
F	0.23	1.53	0.54	0.53
Degrees of freedom	1 and 311	1 and 333	1 and 333	1 and 351

Table 5-13
Test Statistics: Effect of Standard Audit Report on
Assessment of Fraud

Beta	+0.271
Standard error of beta	0.113
F	0.06
Degrees of freedom	1 and 343

the indicated effect of the standard audit report on agreement or disagreement with the statement concerning the absence of fraud, while apparently positive, is not significant at any reasonable level of probability. If investors are concerned about the possible presence of fraud in a reporting company, they are not reassured to any significant degree by an unqualified auditor's report.

Nonstandard Audit Reports

The experiments with nonstandard audit reports used a standard, unqualified audit opinion with an explanatory middle paragraph for the control group and four nonstandard versions of the report for the test groups. None of these nonstandard forms refers in any way to the presence or absence of fraud. Logically these report forms should not affect an investor's assessment of the likelihood of fraud, but of course logic may not rule our beliefs on an issue such as fraud. In table 5-14, the F ratios for the *except for* and *subject to* qualifications and for the disclaimer are not significant, although the effect of the *except for* form approaches significance at a .10 probability level. The adverse opinion, on the other hand, has a very strong and significant effect on the assessment of fraud. On the scale of 0 to 4, an adverse opinion would move the mean scale value down from 2.31 to 1.94.

Table 5-14
Test Statistics: Effect of Nonstandard Audit-Report Forms
on Assessment of Fraud

	Except for Opinion	Subject to Opinion	Adverse Opinion	Disclaimer
Beta	−0.165	−0.197	−0.373	−0.141
Standard error of beta	0.109	0.109	0.109	0.103
F	2.30	0.03	11.61	1.85
Degrees of freedom	1 and 334	1 and 342	1 and 353	1 and 364

Table 5-15
Summary of Tests of Hypotheses: Five Experiments on Seven Behavioral Variables

Behavioral Variable	Experimental Test Variable (Audit-Report Form)				
	Standard Opinion	Except for Opinion	Subject to Opinion	Adverse Opinion	Disclaimer
INCOME PROJECTION	$R_{.10}$	NR	NR	NR	NR
SHARE PRICE ESTIMATE	NR	NR	NR	NR	NR
COMPANY EVALUATION	NR	NR	NR	$R_{.05}$	NR
MANAGEMENT EVALUATION	NR	$R_{.10}$	NR	$R_{.10}$	NR
INVESTMENT DECISION	NR	NR	NR	$R_{.10}$	NR
CONFIDENCE RATING	NR	NR	NR	NR	NR
ASSESSMENT OF FRAUD	NR	NR	NR	$R_{.01}$	NR

R_{α} = null hypothesis is rejected at the indicated level of significance; audit-report form significantly affects behavioral variable.

NR = null hypothesis is not rejected; audit-report form does not significantly affect the behavioral variable.

Tests of Hypotheses

Null hypotheses were stated in chapter 4 as follows:

H_0-1   The addition of a standard audit report to a set of financial statements will have no significant effect on (one of the seven dependent variables).

H_0-2   Replacement of a standard audit report with (one of four non-standard audit reports) will have no significant effect on (one of the seven dependent variables).

H_0-1 produces seven hypotheses, one for each of the dependent variables; while H_0-2 produces 4×7, or 28. Results of these thirty-five tests of hypotheses are summarized in table 5-15. Using .10 as the cutoff probability for determining significance, this table shows that the null hypothesis is not rejected in any case with either the *subject to* opinion or the disclaimer. The standard and *except for* formats produce one rejection each, while the adverse opinion is the "strongest" opinion form with four null-hypothesis rejections.

The implications of these results will be considered in chapter 6.

The Effect of the Auditor's Report on Investor Behavior: Summary and Implications

This study was designed to experimentally test the effects on investor behavior of the independent Certified Public Accountant's audit report. The results may surprise and, perhaps, disappoint some; the audit report has little effect on investor decisions and attitudes.

The conventional wisdom holds that the auditor's report adds credibility to and increases confidence in financial statements. Prior research studies (see chapter 2) have generally failed to support this view. They suggest that the auditor's report is widely ignored and often misunderstood. Studies of the effect of the audit report on stock prices have produced mixed results, with those finding no significant effect outnumbering studies finding a significant market effect. A theoretical analysis (chapter 3) suggests that such mixed results might be expected; the probability that the auditor's intended message will be correctly received may be estimated at less than .33, and the likelihood that the report will produce the desired outcome is probably under .25.

This investigation was designed to overcome several of the disadvantages of prior research based on historical stock-market-price data. The posttest-only-control-group experimental design was chosen as the strongest experimental approach for investigating the effects of different audit-report forms. Five separate experiments were conducted. In the first, subjects were randomly assigned to control and test groups, and both groups were provided with the same financial statements and five-year summary data on the realistic but hypothetical J Company (see appendix A). Statements received by the test group were accompanied by a standard, unqualified "clean" audit opinion; the control group received statements with no audit report. After examining the information packet subjects provided seven behavioral responses, and also provided information on a number of personal characteristics (all listed in appendix A).

For the other four experiments, the control group received the financial statements and summary data accompanied by an unqualified audit opinion that included an additional middle paragraph explaining a lawsuit (generally accepted auditing standards allow an auditor to add such a paragraph to an unqualified opinion to explain or clarify a matter). Four separate test groups received the same financial statements and summary, but with either an *except for* qualified opinion, a *subject to* qualified opinion, an adverse opinion, or a disclaimer; the opinion forms are reproduced in chapter 4. Each of these four report forms included the same explanatory middle paragraph provided, in an unqualified opinion, to the control group. Consequently the only difference between the stimuli provided to the control and the test groups in these four experiments was the wording of the last paragraph of the audit report.

Investors constitute a large and heterogeneous group. To insure an adequate cross section, four groups were sampled: stockholders, security analysts, institutional investors, and other business-persons generally. Access to the first three groups was obtained by mail using lists purchased from a national list company; business-persons in business and economics classes at an urban midwestern university provided the fourth group. (Data on subject characteristics is presented in appendix C.) A total of 1,359 subjects participated in, and were divided among, the five experiments.

Multiple-regression analysis was used to isolate and test the effects of the audit-report forms while controlling for personal characteristics and market conditions. Careful attention was given to the assumptions required for regression analysis, as well as to model specification.

The Standard, Unqualified Audit Report

The standard or clean opinion is the form of audit report usually rendered and the form most commonly seen by investors. This study experimentally investigated the question: Does the standard audit report have any effect on investor behavior? The answer is a qualified no. The addition of a standard audit report to financial statements, in contrast to statements with no accompanying audit report, was found to significantly increase investors' projections of the company's net income for the following year, by some 4.5 percent. The standard opinion had no significant effect, however, on estimates of a fair price for the company's common stock, investors' overall evaluation of the company or its management, the amount invested in the company, investor confidence in the investment decision, or assessment of the likelihood of fraud occurring in the reporting company.

These results are in rather marked contrast to the conventional wisdom that the unqualified audit opinion adds credibility to and increases confidence in financial statements. They are also inconsonant with a number of surveys in which investors indicated that a major purpose of the financial-statement audit is the prevention or detection of fraud. There is some indication, based on the income projections, that investors are somehow more opimistic about a company's future when a standard audit opinion is present, an outcome that could not be predicted from the conventional wisdom. The general lack of audit-report effect on investor attitudes and behavior calls into question the value of the financial-statement audit, at least to investors, and must certainly reinforce existing doubts about the communicative efficacy of the audit report.

Nonstandard Audit Reports

Four nonstandard report forms were investigated: the *except for* opinion, qualified because of noncompliance with generally accepted accounting principles; the *subject to* opinion, qualified on account of uncertainty about the outcome of a future event (in this case an unsettled lawsuit); the adverse opinion rendered because the statements are not fairly presented; and the disclaimer due to excessive uncertainty. Other report forms are possible, and many variations of these four could be constructed. Technically the results of this study apply only to these four forms; while we might expect similar forms to have similar effects, this is a matter for future research and cannot be verified from the present data.

Neither the *subject to* opinion nor the disclaimer produced significant effects on any of the seven behavioral variables. Whether investors do not read these reports, do not understand them, or simply do not react, these results suggest strongly that qualifications or disclaimers for uncertainty have no significant impact on investor behavior. *Once the uncertainty is explained in a middle paragraph, the investor does not appear to care about the auditor's opinion itself; it could just as well be unqualified.*

The *except for* opinion produced only one significant effect: the evaluation of the qualification of company management is reduced significantly. Given the presence of the explanatory middle paragraph, the auditor's opinion qualification makes no significant difference in the investor's income projection, estimate of a fair price for the company's common stock, overall evaluation of the company, investment decision, confidence in the investment decision, or assessment of the likelihood of fraud.

Why does the *except for* qualification have a negative effect on the investor's evaluation of management? While any answer would be only speculative since this question is not addressed in the present study, one explanation was offered by several investors: "Any management that can't clean up its financial statements well enough to avoid a qualified audit report can't be too sharp."

The adverse opinion was the only report form that produced several significant reactions. Even when the matter of concern is described fully in an explanatory paragraph, the addition of the auditor's opinion that the financial statements are not fairly presented has a significant negative effect on investors' overall evaluations of the company and of management, greatly increases investors' concerns about the possibility of fraud, and results in a 17 percent reduction in the amount that investors are willing to put into the company's stock. The adverse audit opinion has negative consequences for the reporting company; substantial investment in accounting system improvements may be justified to avoid such a report.

This study represents a major effort to assess directly the impact of the audit report in its several versions. While human behavior is highly variable and therefore difficult to account for, the controls introduced in this research provide a basis for confidence in the conclusion that, with the exception of the adverse opinion, audit reports have, at best, a very limited effect on investors. Even the effects found may be exaggerated, however:

1. In testing 35 hypotheses (five report forms and seven behavioral variables), three to four significant effects (at a .10 level of significance) could occur due simply to random variation. Of the six significant effects found, only two (involving the adverse opinion) were significant at a level of .05 or less.
2. Since the amount of information provided to subjects in the experiment was limited, and certainly less than that available when one is evaluating a real company, the impact of each item of information provided, including the audit report, may be amplified.

Independent audits of financial statements by Certified Public Accountants cost reporting companies in the United States billions of dollars annually. Does this great cost produce concomitant benefits (other than to the CPAs)? We are a long way from answering this question, but, as noted earlier, the results of this study raise serious questions about the value to investors of the present auditor's report on financial statements.

A Theory to Explain the Results

On casual examination it is difficult to understand why audit reports do not significantly affect investor behavior. The rationale for independent, expert attestation to the fairness of corporate financial reporting seems to be straightforward and sensible. Corporations seek capital from investors. Investors need information about the corporation before investing. In providing this information, corporate management may be tempted to exaggerate, mislead, cover up—and may simply err as well. To facilitate active capital markets and industrial growth, the SEC and stock exchanges require companies to provide financial reports on which a Certified Public Accountant has expressed an opinion.

This audit report should be of great interest to investors, but it is not. It appears, instead, to be widely ignored.

Why is the audit report, which should be so important and which costs reporting corporations so much, generally ignored? There are at least two possible explanations, which can be called the surprise-value hypothesis and the investor-conditioning hypothesis.

The hypothesis of surprise value is related to the efficient-markets theory. This theory holds that markets are efficient with respect to the assimilation of information into market actions through buy, sell, and hold decisions. Published financial statements will contain no new information of value to the market, data reported in these statements will have been received by investors well before release of the statements, and that data will already have been integrated into investment decisions (and into share prices). If investors obtain and assimilate all the data contained in financial statements and the accompanying audit report including any uncertainty or noncompliance with generally accepted accounting principles, before the publication of the statements, then we might expect the published statements and audit report to be largely ignored. That is, the document containing the financial statements and audit report might be ignored, but the data contained therein would have reached the market previously and may have had significant value to investors when first received. Under such circumstances, investors could have gotten into the habit of ignoring the published audit report, and this could account for the general absence of audit-report effect on investors in the present study.

This explanation can hold only so long as the published financial statements and audit report agree with information previously given currency in the marketplace—as long as the published statements contain no surprises. This appears to be generally the case, due perhaps to such factors as the ability of investment researchers and analysts to obtain timely factual information, legislation that seeks to prevent profiting from insider information, laws proscribing fraud and deception, and the persuasive effect of the independent auditor in inducing full and truthful disclosure. If the present situation were to change and published reports were to contain frequent surprises, we would very possibly find that the statements and auditors' opinions do indeed contain information of value to investors and the results of a study such as the one reported here could be significantly different.

The hypothesis of investor conditioning is based on the standardization of audit-report wording and format. The wording of the standard, unqualified audit report is prescribed by the American Institute of CPAs, and most CPA firms follow this wording precisely. Even qualified reports are made as uniform as possible.

By standardizing the audit report, the accounting profession may have insured that it will be uninteresting. The reader has apparently been conditioned to expect no surprises, and so does not read the audit report. Even when the auditor's report is modified or qualified, any but the most knowledgable reader would have to do a line by line comparison with the standard wording to find the changes.

In summary, the hypothesis of surprise value holds that the auditor's report has value only insofar as it has the potential to surprise, to reveal important information not previously known to the market—and such surprises rarely occur. The related hypothesis of investor conditioning holds that investors have been conditioned, through standardization of audit-report wording and format, to expect the report to be of no interest. Together these hypotheses may at least partially explain why, as was found in this study, the auditor's report has very little effect on investor behavior.

Future Implications and a Proposal

"Since 1949 [the auditor's] opinion on financial statements has fossilized in esoteric language." (Sale, p. 82) The form and wording of the auditor's report was studied thoroughly by the Commission on Auditors' Responsibilities, which recommended that the report be revised and lengthened, but that the wording for each paragraph remain standardized. The Auditing Standards Board of the AICPA took up the commission's recommendations and proposed several revisions in the standard wording, but after extensive debate the board concluded that "the current auditor's standard report could not be improved enough to warrant the cost of change." ("ASB Opts to Keep Current Auditor's Report" 1981)

Following all this study and struggle, it is evident that the accounting profession is not going to change the standard wording of the auditor's report in the foreseeable future. This may be just as well, since the hypotheses of conditional value and of investor conditioning suggest that investors will continue to ignore audit reports *as long as they are standardized* and are, therefore, neither surprising nor interesting.

What will happen if the audit report is not changed? While investors represent one of the major audiences for audit reports, it appears from this study that investors generally fail to react to these reports. If investors were paying directly for the auditor's opinion, they would undoubtedly demand either some sort of change in the report so it would provide useful information, or they would stop buying, that is, fire the auditors. Since the demand for financial-statement audits is largely indirect, imposed by the SEC and by stock exchanges instead of by the target audiences, a number of years may pass before the apparent investor indifference produces an examination of the need for audits. In light of recent congressional attention to the accounting profession and the current emphasis in Washington on deregulation, this examination, when it comes, may result in a reduction in the requirements for independent audits of financial statements.

Such a reduction might have a positive social effect if the original value of the audit is now obtained to a significant extent through other means, such as probing and reporting by more sophisticated business journalists; legislation dealing with fraud, misleading advertising, and profiting from inside information; more aggressive and competitive investment researchers and analysts; the reliance of a substantial body of investors on overall market performance instead of on fundamental analysis of company data; the greater role of institutional investors, who need less protection than the "Aunt Jane" investor; all coupled with efficient markets that quickly integrate information into security prices and investment decisions. But a reduction in present requirements for audits could have a negative social effect if the present audit report has the potential, based on the evidence and information gained by the CPA in the course of the audit, to provide significant information of value to investors—information that is apparently not now being provided, judging from the lack of audit-report effect on investor behavior.

To maximize its value, the audit report should be changed to allow for the provision of additional information to investors—information that is not provided by a standardized report. *All standardized wording should be dropped; the auditor's report should be composed anew, "from scratch," for each audit.* This will be recognized as a proposal for a return to something akin to the long-form report.

An audit of a company whose securities are traded publicly requires hundreds or thousands of hours of planning, investigation, observation, testing, and evaluation. It is surely not unreasonable to expect that the report based on this great effort reflect some original thought, and that it literally provide the auditor's personal (or the CPA firm's collective) professional opinion of the subject financial statements. Instead of using stock phrases, the auditor should clearly indicate the responsibility taken for the statements. Instead of presenting a standardized opinion paragraph with practically meaningless phrases such as "present fairly" and "generally accepted accounting principles," the auditor should express a complete and personal opinion, as a professional, on the adequacy and accuracy with which the financial statements present the company's financial position, results of operations, and changes in financial position. For example, a CPA who believes that a formula depreciation method fails to accurately reflect the loss of utility in fixed assets should say so, instead of merely reporting that the statements conform to generally accepted accounting principles. If CPAs are truly professionals with all the skill and knowledge that we claim, then surely we can say what we think and what we mean as a result of an audit of financial statements. Let the marketplace weed out the CPA who cannot produce a clear, informative, unbiased, and unexaggerated report. Let the SEC, stock exchanges, bankers, and indeed client companies refuse to accept audit reports that are overly qualified, excessively ambiguous, convoluted, unclear.

The results of this study indicate that the auditor's report has little effect on investor behavior, possibly because of the standardized format and wording of the report. This situation has the potential to produce a significant reduction in the requirements for financial-statement audits, a result that may not be in the interests of the investment community and of society. Consequently, it is proposed that the standardized audit-report be eliminated, and that the CPA be allowed to apply genuine professional judgment to produce an audit report, based on the circumstances and conclusions of each audit, that can provide information of real value to investors.

Appendix A:
Experimental Stimuli

QUESTIONNAIRE

As you know, complete and serious responses are necessary in a study such as this to maintain statistical validity. Please give each question careful consideration; do not leave any blank. While your thoughtful participation is very important, individual responses will be kept completely confidential.

1. How many years experience have you had in working in or with business organizations? (Do not count government, military, public educational, or social service organizations; do include retail stores, manufacturers, distributors, profit seeking service organizations such as insurance companies, and other business firms of all types and sizes.) Round your answer to the nearest whole year.

_____ years

2. Approximately how many semester and/or quarter hours of college courses have you had in accounting, if any. (Do not include data processing or computer programming courses.)

Semester hours _____
Quarter hours _____

How many hours in finance and investments courses, if any?

Semester hours _____
Quarter hours _____

3. How many years of college work, including graduate work, have you completed? Please round your answer to the nearest whole number. (If some of your academic work was part-time, use full year equivalents.)

_____ years

4. What is the approximate market value today of your investments in:

Corporate stocks $_____

Corporate bonds $_____

Other securities, including government bonds, savings accounts, certificates of deposit, etc. (do not include insurance policies) $_____

5. Please estimate the Dow Jones Industrial Average as of the close of business today. (Even if you have no clear idea, give the best estimate you can; do not leave blank. Please do not, however, refer to a newspaper or other source.)

_____

6. Approximately how many times have you bought or sold corporate stocks within the past two years?

_____

7. Do you evaluate stocks or advise investors (check one)

(a) frequently _____
(b) occasionally _____
(c) rarely _____
(d) never _____

8. What is your sex?

Male _____   Female _____

9. What is your age?

_____

10. Since this study is being conducted across the nation, it will be helpful if you indicate the city (or town) and state in which you are located at this moment.

_____

[Please turn this page over for the remaining questions.]

Also, please indicate in a few words the *setting* or circumstances in which the experiment is being administered. (For instance, "stockholders' meeting", "my office", "professional conference", etc.).

_____

_____

11. Please indicate today's date.   Month _____ Day _____ Year _____

The following questions relate to the attached information on the J Company. Ordinarily you might seek additional information before making decisions or answering questions such as these about a company. Since this is an experiment, it is necessary for you to base your responses only on the attached information along with your own general knowledge and attitudes. While some of the questions may be frustrating and you may feel you have insufficient information or knowledge, please respond as thoughtfully as you can to *all* of the questions; do not leave any blank.

1. Assume you are managing a new investment fund for a group of shareholders whose instructions to you are to (1) invest only in common stocks of companies listed on the New York Stock Exchange; (2) seek a reasonable balance between income and growth; and (3) invest the entire fund balance of $100,000 immediately. (Please do your best to play this role even if it is an unfamiliar one for you.) Diversification is not a goal; you may invest all of the fund in a single company or diversify widely, as you like. Assume the J Company, whose statements are attached, is listed on the New York Stock Exchange. At a price per share of $12, how much, if any, of the $100,000 would you invest in J Company stock? (Please respond with a dollar amount, not a percentage.)

$_____

2. This is a hard question but an important one. Think about your degree of confidence in the preceding answer concerning the amount to be invested in J Company stock. Do you feel fairly confident about the correctness of your answer in terms of the three specified investment objectives, or are you pretty uncertain. Using a scale of 0 to 10, with 10 signifying complete confidence and 0 signifying no confidence at all, please indicate your degree of confidence in the preceding answer.

(answer with a whole number from 0 to 10) _____

3. What is your estimate of a fair price per share for J Company common stock? (Round your estimate to the nearest dollar.)

$_____

4. Please estimate, to the nearest thousand, the total dollar amount of J Company's net income after taxes for the coming year (19X6), assuming no significant changes in capital structure, markets, products, personnel, or operating procedures.

$_____,000

5. Please indicate the extent to which you agree or disagree with each of the following statements by placing an "X" in one of the five segments of the scale. For example, if you really like apple pie, you would respond to the sample statement as indicated.

Sample: Apple pie is good.

Strongly Agree | X | | | | | Strongly Disagree

a. It appears that the management of J Company is well qualified.

Strongly Agree | | | | | | Strongly Disagree

b.. It appears that the risk of fraud in the J Company is low.

c. J Company is a successful company.

d. This is a good time to be investing in the stock market. (This refers to common stock investments generally and not just to the J Company.)

Thank you very much for your help.

DESCRIPTION OF THE J COMPANY

The J Company is incorporated in the state of Delaware and has been engaged in the manufacture of household products for fifty-two years. The company's growth since a post World War II surge has been continuous and strong. To diversify its household product base, J Company purchased 100% of a small sporting goods manufacturer fifteen years ago.

Household manufacturing includes large and small kitchen appliances, furniture, and kitchen utensils. Approximately 18% of gross annual sales are industrial products. The industrial products division adds proportionately to profitability, since lower gross profit margins are offset by low selling and administrative expenses.

J Company has a history of continuous dividend payments for twenty-three years. The number of shares outstanding has remained relatively constant in recent years with no treasury stock repurchase policies.

The outlook for the coming fiscal year is good. The management goals are for minimizing costs and pursuing opportunities which will enhance profitability, growth, and market diversification.

J COMPANY - CONSOLIDATED BALANCE SHEET

	December 31 ($000 omitted)	
	19X5	19X4
ASSETS		
Current Assets:		
Cash	$ 18,200	$ 17,900
Marketable securities	2,200	2,100
Accounts and notes receivable, less allowance for uncollectible accounts of $1,099,000 and $1,067,000	53,869	52,300
Inventories, at lower of cost (first-in, first-out) or market		
Raw materials	15,500	15,200
Finished goods	125,300	123,900
Total Current Assets	$215,069	$211,400
Property, plant and equipment, at cost less accumulated depreciation of $19,600,000 and $17,300,000.	66,100	61,100
	$281,169	$272,500
LIABILITIES AND STOCKHOLDERS EQUITY		
Current Liabilities:		
Notes payable	$ 22,000	$ 24,500
Accounts payable	66,368	67,831
Income taxes payable	1,564	1,434
Total Current Liabilities	$ 89,932	$ 93,765
Long-Term Debt (see Note 2)	$ 63,000	$ 53,000
Stockholders' Equity:		
Capital stock, par value $1.00 (authorized 10,000,000 shares, issued and outstanding 7,000,000 shares)	$ 7,000	$ 7,000
Additional paid-in capital	30,000	30,000
Retained earnings	91,237	88,735
Total Stockholders' Equity	$128,237	$125,735
	$281,169	$272,500

The accompanying notes are an integral part of this statement.

J COMPANY · CONSOLIDATED STATEMENT OF INCOME AND RETAINED EARNINGS

	Year Ended December 31 ($000 omitted)			
	19X5		19X4	
NET SALES	$400,771	100%	$389,098	100%
Other income	110	–	107	–
	$400,881		$389,205	
COSTS AND EXPENSES (including provisions for				
depreciation of $2,300,000 and $2,000,000)				
Cost of sales	$292,563	73%	$289,000	74%
Selling, general and administrative expenses	81,146	20%	74,700	19%
Interest expense	8,100	2%	7,998	2%
Income taxes	7,820	2%	7,172	2%
	$389,629	97%	$378,870	97%
NET INCOME	$ 11,252	3%	$ 10,335	3%
RETAINED EARNINGS AT BEGINNING OF PERIOD	88,735		86,100	
Dividends paid (19X5: $1.25 per share; 19X4: $1.10				
per share)	(8,750)		(7,700)	
RETAINED EARNINGS AT END OF PERIOD	$ 91,237		$ 88,735	
NET INCOME PER SHARE	$1.61		$1.48	

The accompanying notes are an integral part of this statement.

J COMPANY · CONSOLIDATED STATEMENT OF CHANGES IN FINANCIAL POSITION

	Year Ended December 31 ($000 omitted)	
	19X5	19X4
SOURCE OF FUNDS		
Net income	$ 11,252	$ 10,335
Expense not requiring outlay of working		
capital ·· depreciation	2,300	2,000
Provided from Operations	$ 13,552	$ 12,335
Proceeds from long-term borrowings	10,000	–
Total Funds Provided	$ 23,552	$ 12,335
USE OF FUNDS		
Cash dividends	$ 8,750	$ 7,700
Net additions to property, plant and		
equipment	7,300	2,600
Total Funds Used	$ 16,050	$ 10,300
Net Increase in Working Capital	$ 7,502	$ 2,035

The accompanying notes are an integral part of this statement.

J COMPANY - FIVE-YEAR STATISTICAL SUMMARY ($000 omitted)

	19X5	19X4	19X3	19X2	19X1
SUMMARY OF OPERATIONS					
Net sales	$400,771	$389,098	$377,765	$366,762	$356,080
Income before income taxes	19,072	17,507	16,045	13,657	13,394
Taxes on income	7,820	7,172	6,357	5,528	5,561
Net income	11,252	10,335	9,688	8,129	7,833
Percent to net sales	2.8	2.7	2.6	2.2	2.2
Cash dividends paid	8,750	7,700	7,105	5,439	5,218
Depreciation	2,300	2,000	2,000	1,700	1,800
Capital expenditures	7,300	2,600	8,500	2,100	1,900
YEAR-END FINANCIAL DATA					
Current assets	$215,069	$211,400	$203,687	$205,506	$202,733
Current liabilities	89,932	93,765	88,087	92,989	90,506
Working capital	125,137	117,635	115,600	112,517	112,227
Ratio of current assets to current liabilities	2.39:1	2.25:1	2.31:1	2.21:1	2.24:1
Plant and equipment - net	66,100	61,100	60,500	54,000	53,600
Total assets	281,169	272,500	264,187	259,506	256,333
Long-term debt	63,000	53,000	53,000	46,000	48,000
Stockholders' equity	128,237	125,735	123,100	120,517	117,827
Shares outstanding at year-end	7,000,000	7,000,000	7,000,000	7,000,000	7,000,000
PER SHARE					
Net income	$1.61	$1.48	1.38	$1.16	$1.12
Dividends	1.25	1.10	1.02	.78	.75
Stockholders' equity	18.32	17.96	17.59	17.22	16.83

The accompanying notes are an integral part of this statement.

NOTES TO CONSOLIDATED FINANCIAL STATEMENTS

1. **Summary of Significant Accounting Policies**

Principles of Consolidation:

Consolidated financial statements include the accounts of the parent company and a wholly owned domestic subsidiary. There are no foreign subsidiaries.

Inventories:

Inventories are valued at the lower of cost (first-in, first-out method) or market.

Property, Plant and Equipment, and Depreciation:

Property, plant and equipment is recorded on the basis of cost. Depreciation is based on estimated service lives of the respective classes of property and is computed on the straight-line method.

2. **Long-Term Debt**

Long-term debt consisted of:

	19X5	19X4
8½% Notes due 19X8	$53,000,000	$53,000,000
10½% Subordinated Debentures due 19X9	10,000,000	—

NOTES TO CONSOLIDATED FINANCIAL STATEMENTS

1. Summary of Significant Accounting Policies

Principles of Consolidation:

Consolidated financial statements include the accounts of the parent company and a wholly owned domestic subsidiary. There are no foreign subsidiaries.

Inventories:

Inventories are valued at the lower of cost (first-in, first-out method) or market.

Property, Plant and Equipment, and Depreciation:

Property, plant and equipment is recorded on the basis of cost. Depreciation is based on estimated service lives of the respective classes of property and is computed on the straight-line method.

2. Long-Term Debt

Long-term debt consisted of:

	19X5	19X4
8½% Notes due 19X8	$53,000,000	$53,000,000
10½% Subordinated Debentures due 19X9	10,000,000	—

AUDITOR'S OPINION

We have examined the consolidated balance sheets of J Company as of December 31, 19X5 and 19X4 and the statements of consolidated income, retained earnings, and changes in financial position for the years then ended. Our examinations were made in accordance with generally accepted auditing standards and, accordingly, included such tests of the accounting records and such other auditing procedures as we considered necessary in the circumstances.

In our opinion, the financial statements referred to above present fairly the consolidated financial position of J Company as of December 31, 19X5 and 19X4 and the consolidated results of its operations and the changes in its financial position for the years then ended, in conformity with generally accepted accounting principles applied on a consistent basis.

Center City
U.S.A.

Smith and Jones
Certified Public Accountants

NOTES TO CONSOLIDATED FINANCIAL STATEMENTS

1. Summary of Significant Accounting Policies

Principles of Consolidation:

Consolidated financial statements include the accounts of the parent company and a wholly owned domestic subsidiary. There are no foreign subsidiaries.

Inventories:

Inventories are valued at the lower of cost (first-in, first-out method) or market.

Property, Plant and Equipment, and Depreciation:

Property, plant and equipment is recorded on the basis of cost. Depreciation is based on estimated service lives of the respective classes of property and is computed on the straight-line method.

2. Long-Term Debt

Long-term debt consisted of:

	19X5	19X4
8½% Notes due 19X8	$53,000,000	$53,000,000
10½% Subordinated Debentures due 19X9	10,000,000	—

AUDITOR'S OPINION

We have examined the consolidated balance sheets of J Company as of December 31, 19X5 and 19X4 and the statements of consolidated income, retained earnings, and changes in financial position for the years then ended. Our examinations were made in accordance with generally accepted auditing standards and, accordingly, included such tests of the accounting records and such other auditing procedures as we considered necessary in the circumstances.

During the current year the Company became a defendant in a lawsuit alleging infringement of certain patent rights and claiming royalties and punitive damages. The Company has filed a counter action, and preliminary hearings and discovery proceedings on both actions are in progress. Company officers and counsel believe the Company has a good chance of prevailing, but the ultimate outcome of the lawsuits cannot presently be determined. No provision for any liability that may result has been made in the financial statements, nor do the financial statements contain any disclosure of this matter.

In our opinion, the financial statements referred to above present fairly the consolidated financial position of J Company as of December 31, 19X5 and 19X4 and the consolidated results of its operations and the changes in its financial position for the years then ended, in conformity with generally accepted accounting principles applied on a consistent basis.

Center City   Smith and Jones
U.S.A.   Certified Public Accountants

NOTES TO CONSOLIDATED FINANCIAL STATEMENTS

1. Summary of Significant Accounting Policies

Principles of Consolidation:

Consolidated financial statements include the accounts of the parent company and a wholly owned domestic subsidiary. There are no foreign subsidiaries.

Inventories:

Inventories are valued at the lower of cost (first-in, first-out method) or market.

Property, Plant and Equipment, and Depreciation:

Property, plant and equipment is recorded on the basis of cost. Depreciation is based on estimated service lives of the respective classes of property and is computed on the straight-line method.

2. Long-Term Debt

Long-term debt consisted of:

	19X5	19X4
8½% Notes due 19X8	$53,000,000	$53,000,000
10½% Subordinated Debentures due 19X9	10,000,000	—

AUDITOR'S OPINION

We have examined the consolidated balance sheets of J Company as of December 31, 19X5 and 19X4 and the statements of consolidated income, retained earnings, and changes in financial position for the years then ended. Our examinations were made in accordance with generally accepted auditing standards and, accordingly, included such tests of the accounting records and such other auditing procedures as we considered necessary in the circumstances.

During the current year the Company became a defendant in a lawsuit alleging infringement of certain patent rights and claiming royalties and punitive damages. The Company has filed a counter action, and preliminary hearings and discovery proceedings on both actions are in progress. Company officers and counsel believe the Company has a good chance of prevailing, but the ultimate outcome of the lawsuits cannot presently be determined. No provision for any liability that may result has been made in the financial statements, nor do the financial statements contain any disclosure of this matter.

In our opinion, except for the failure to disclose the pending lawsuit in the 19X5 financial statements as discussed in the preceding paragraph, the financial statements referred to above present fairly the consolidated financial position of J Company as of December 31, 19X5 and 19X4 and the consolidated results of its operations and the changes in its financial position for the years then ended, in conformity with generally accepted accounting principles applied on a consistent basis.

Center City   Smith and Jones
U.S.A.   Certified Public Accountants

NOTES TO CONSOLIDATED FINANCIAL STATEMENTS

1. Summary of Significant Accounting Policies

Principles of Consolidation:

    Consolidated financial statements include the accounts of the parent company and a wholly owned domestic subsidiary. There are no foreign subsidiaries.

Inventories:

    Inventories are valued at the lower of cost (first-in, first-out method) or market.

Property, Plant and Equipment, and Depreciation:

    Property, plant and equipment is recorded on the basis of cost. Depreciation is based on estimated service lives of the respective classes of property and is computed on the straight-line method.

2. Long-Term Debt

Long-term debt consisted of:

	19X5	19X4
8½% Notes due 19X8	$53,000,000	$53,000,000
10½% Subordinated Debentures due 19X9	10,000,000	—

AUDITOR'S OPINION

We have examined the consolidated balance sheets of J Company as of December 31, 19X5 and 19X4 and the statements of consolidated income, retained earnings, and changes in financial position for the years then ended. Our examinations were made in accordance with generally accepted auditing standards and, accordingly, included such tests of the accounting records and such other auditing procedures as we considered necessary in the circumstances.

During the current year the Company became a defendant in a lawsuit alleging infringement of certain patent rights and claiming royalties and punitive damages. The Company has filed a counter action, and preliminary hearings and discovery proceedings on both actions are in progress. Company officers and counsel believe the Company has a good chance of prevailing, but the ultimate outcome of the lawsuits cannot presently be determined. No provision for any liability that may result has been made in the financial statements, nor do the financial statements contain any disclosure of this matter.

In our opinion, subject to the effects, if any, on the 19X5 financial statements of the ultimate resolution of the matter discussed in the preceding paragraph, the financial statements referred to above present fairly the consolidated financial position of J Company as of December 31, 19X5 and 19X4 and the consolidated results of its operations and the changes in its financial position for the years then ended, in conformity with generally accepted accounting principles applied on a consistent basis.

Center City
U.S.A.

Smith and Jones
Certified Public Accountants

NOTES TO CONSOLIDATED FINANCIAL STATEMENTS

1. Summary of Significant Accounting Policies

Principles of Consolidation:

   Consolidated financial statements include the accounts of the parent company and a wholly owned domestic subsidiary. There are no foreign subsidiaries.

Inventories:

   Inventories are valued at the lower of cost (first-in, first-out method) or market.

Property, Plant and Equipment, and Depreciation:

   Property, plant and equipment is recorded on the basis of cost. Depreciation is based on estimated service lives of the respective classes of property and is computed on the straight-line method.

2. Long-Term Debt

Long-term debt consisted of:

	19X5	19X4
8½% Notes due 19X8	$53,000,000	$53,000,000
10½% Subordinated Debentures due 19X9	10,000,000	—

AUDITOR'S OPINION

   We have examined the consolidated balance sheets of J Company as of December 31, 19X5 and 19X4 and the statements of consolidated income, retained earnings, and changes in financial position for the years then ended. Our examinations were made in accordance with generally accepted auditing standards and, accordingly, included such tests of the accounting records and such other auditing procedures as we considered necessary in the circumstances.

   During the current year the Company became a defendant in a lawsuit alleging infringement of certain patent rights and claiming royalties and punitive damages. The Company has filed a counter action, and preliminary hearings and discovery proceedings on both actions are in progress. Company officers and counsel believe the Company has a good chance of prevailing, but the ultimate outcome of the lawsuits cannot presently be determined. No provision for any liability that may result has been made in the financial statements, nor do the financial statements contain any disclosure of this matter.

   In our opinion, the 19X4 financial statements present fairly the consolidated financial position of J Company as of December 31, 19X4 and the consolidated results of its operations and the changes in its financial position for the year then ended, in conformity with generally accepted accounting principles applied on a consistent basis.

   Further, in our opinion, because of the failure to disclose the lawsuit referred to above, the 19X5 financial statements do not present fairly, in conformity with generally accepted accounting principles, the consolidated financial position of J Company as of December 31, 19X5 or the consolidated results of its operations and changes in its financial position for the year then ended.

Center City   Smith and Jones
U.S.A.   Certified Public Accountants

NOTES TO CONSOLIDATED FINANCIAL STATEMENTS

1. Summary of Significant Accounting Policies

Principles of Consolidation:

Consolidated financial statements include the accounts of the parent company and a wholly owned domestic subsidiary. There are no foreign subsidiaries.

Inventories:

Inventories are valued at the lower of cost (first-in, first-out method) or market.

Property, Plant and Equipment, and Depreciation:

Property, plant and equipment is recorded on the basis of cost. Depreciation is based on estimated service lives of the respective classes of property and is computed on the straight-line method.

2. Long-Term Debt

Long-term debt consisted of:

	19X5	19X4
8½% Notes due 19X8	$53,000,000	$53,000,000
10½% Subordinated Debentures due 19X9	10,000,000	—

AUDITOR'S OPINION

We have examined the consolidated balance sheets of J Company as of December 31, 19X5 and 19X4 and the statements of consolidated income, retained earnings, and changes in financial position for the years then ended. Our examinations were made in accordance with generally accepted auditing standards and, accordingly, included such tests of the accounting records and such other auditing procedures as we considered necessary in the circumstances.

During the current year the Company became a defendant in a lawsuit alleging infringement of certain patent rights and claiming royalties and punitive damages. The Company has filed a counter action, and preliminary hearings and discovery proceedings on both actions are in progress. Company officers and counsel believe the Company has a good chance of prevailing, but the ultimate outcome of the lawsuits cannot presently be determined. No provision for any liablity that may result has been made in the financial statements, nor do the financial statements contain any disclosure of this matter.

In our opinion, the 19X4 financial statements present fairly the consolidated financial position of J Company as of December 31, 19X4 and the consolidated results of its operations and the changes in its financial position for the year then ended, in conformity with generally accepted accounting principles applied on a consistent basis.

Because of the uncertainty associated with the lawsuit referred to above, we are not able to express, and we do not express, an opinion on the 19X5 financial statements.

Center City
U.S.A.

Smith and Jones
Certified Public Accountants

Appendix B:
Summary of Dependent and Independent Variables

The following variables were found to significantly increase the multiple coefficient of determination (R^2) in one or more of the estimating equations.

EXPERIENCE—Years of experience working in organizations

YEARS OF COLLEGE—Number of equivalent full years of college work, part time and full time, graduate and undergraduate

DJIA ESTIMATE ERROR—Absolute amount of the difference between subject's estimate and the actual Dow Jones Industrial Average

STOCK TRANSACTIONS—Square root of number of times corporate stocks were bought or sold by the subject during the past two years (square root used to reduce effect of extreme values)

STOCK EVALUATIONS—Frequency with which the subject evaluates stocks or advises investors (0 = never; 1 = rarely; 2 = occasionally; 3 = frequently)

SEX—(0 = male; 1 = female)

AGE

ACTUAL DJIA—Closing Dow Jones Industrial Average for the date of participation in the experiment (range: 765-853)

INVESTMENT ATTITUDE—Subject's indication of agreement on a scale of 0-4 with the statement, "This is a good time to be investing in the stock market" (0 = strongly disagree; 4 = strongly agree)

TOTAL CREDITS—Sum of semester credit hours in both accounting and finance or investment courses (quarter hours were converted to semester hours)

HOURSX—Square root of (ACCOUNTING HOURS × FINANCE HOURS)

YEARSX—Square root of (EXPERIENCE × AGE)

In addition, dummy variables were used to represent subject category (SECURITY ANALYSTS, INSTITUTIONAL INVESTORS, STOCKHOLDERS, OTHER BUSINESS PERSONS) and audit-opinion form (OPINION); dummy variables are coded 1 when the condition is present, and 0 otherwise.

Dependent variables in the equations are

INCOME PROJECTION—Subject's estimate of J Company net income for the coming year, in thousands of dollars

SHARE PRICE ESTIMATE—Estimate of a fair price for J Company stock

COMPANY EVALUATION—Agreement on a scale of 0-4 with the statement, "J Company is a successful company" (0 = strongly disagree; 4 = strongly agree)

MANAGEMENT EVALUATION—Agreement on a scale of 0-4 with the statement, "It appears that the management of J Company is well qualified" (0 = strongly disagree; 4 = strongly agree)

INVESTMENT DECISION—Amount subject would invest in the hypothetical J Company out of a fund of $100,000 that must be invested immediately in New York Stock Exchange listed companies (range: $0-$100,000)

CONFIDENCE RATING—Subject's assessment of his or her confidence in the INVESTMENT DECISION on a scale of 0-10 (0 = no confidence at all; 10 = complete confidence)

ASSESSMENT OF FRAUD—Agreement on a scale of 0-4 with the statement, "It appears that the risk of fraud in the J Company is low" (0 = strongly disagree; 4 = strongly agree)

Appendix C:
Characteristics
of Subjects

Four groups of subjects were used—shareholders, security analysts, institutional investors, and others representing the general business community. The first three groups were accessed by mail, while the fourth group was accessed in classroom settings (primarily graduate and upper-division classes) at Wichita State University.

Complete statistics on subject characteristics are presented in tables C-1 through C-13. Data for security analysts and for institutional investors are presented separately and also combined as "professional investors."

Table C-1
Age of Subjects

	Mean	Standard Deviation	n*
Security analysts	45.98	12.22	173
Institutional investors	47.63	10.70	212
Professional investors	46.88	11.43	385
Stockholders	52.86	13.17	394
Other business-persons	26.52	6.57	542
All	40.31	15.65	1,321

*n = number responding on this particular item, which may be fewer than the total number participating as subjects.

Table C-2
Years of Business Experience

	Mean	Standard Deviation	n
Security analysts	20.62	11.07	179
Institutional investors	22.05	10.88	222
Professional investors	21.41	10.97	401
Stockholders	20.78	15.40	392
Other business-persons	3.94	4.09	543
All	14.13	13.55	1,336

Table C-3
Years of College

	Mean	Standard Deviation	n
Security analysts	5.60	1.47	177
Institutional investors	5.01	1.47	221
Professional investors	5.27	1.50	398
Stockholders	4.44	2.57	392
Other business-persons	4.04	1.47	530
All	4.53	1.94	1,320

Table C-4
Credit Hours in Accounting

	Mean	Standard Deviation	n
Security analysts	11.17	8.83	165
Institutional investors	20.91	14.67	211
Professional investors	16.59	13.36	376
Stockholders	5.70	9.63	375
Other business-persons	9.68	8.09	499
All	10.58	11.22	1,250

Table C-5
Credit Hours in Finance

	Mean	Standard Deviation	n
Security analysts	15.28	13.34	165
Institutional investors	10.04	9.02	210
Professional investors	12.33	11.40	375
Stockholders	4.03	6.19	374
Other business-persons	2.90	3.53	478
All	6.13	8.57	1,227

Table C-6
Market Value of Stocks

	Mean	Standard Deviation	n
Security analysts	1,034,360	2,767,004	163
Institutional investors	704,785	2,187,357	214
Professional investors	845,039	2,453,639	377
Stockholders	148,577	283,754	391
Other business-persons	1,092	4,579	514
All	294,914	1,388,213	1,282

Table C-7
Market Value of Bonds

	Mean	Standard Deviation	n
Security analysts	853,104	2,751,898	163
Institutional investors	600,081	2,241,834	214
Professional investors	707,601	2,471,699	377
Stockholders	19,885	47,531	387
Other business-persons	245	1,896	494
All	218,831	1,391,471	1,258

Table C-8
Market Value of Other Securities

	Mean	Standard Deviation	n
Security analysts	888,994	2,721,827	162
Institutional investors	503,122	2,001,227	214
Professional investors	665,834	2,337,524	376
Stockholders	61,560	124,601	392
Other business-persons	2,680	5,812	528
All	213,912	1,296,346	1,296

Table C-9
Number of Stock Transactions in Past Two Years

	Mean	Standard Deviation	n
Security analysts	70.05	177.58	169
Institutional investors	19.65	76.58	217
Professional investors	41.72	132.96	386
Stockholders	26.67	44.41	401
Other business-persons	0.85	3.36	533
All	20.64	77.86	1,320

Table C-10
Frequency of Stock Evaluations
(Percentages)

	Frequently	Occasionally	Rarely	Never
Security analysts	76.4	14.0	7.9	1.7
Institutional investors	25.1	28.3	26.0	20.6
Professional investors	47.9	21.9	18.0	12.2
Stockholders	43.5	27.5	14.0	15.0
Other business-persons	1.1	10.6	18.3	70.0
All	27.6	19.0	16.9	36.5

Table C-11
Familiarity with Dow Jones Industrial Average
(Actual DJIA – Estimated DJIA)

	Mean	Standard Deviation	n
Security analysts	1.1	8.9	165
Institutional investors	−0.9	77.0	214
Professional investors	0.1	58.1	379
Stockholders	−3.8	62.7	367
Other business-persons	−255.6	366.0	477
All	−100.8	264.1	1,223

Table C-12
Investment Attitude (Agreement with statement, "This is a good time to be investing in the stock market")

	Percentage					Mean[a]
	Strongly Agree				Strongly Disagree	
Security analysts	20.2 :	31.5 :	18.5 :	18.5 :	11.2	2.31
Institutional investors	14.3 :	30.4 :	19.2 :	23.2 :	12.9	2.10
Professional investors	16.9 :	30.8 :	18.9 :	21.1 :	12.2	2.19
Stockholders	19.0 :	23.7 :	27.7 :	17.7 :	12.0	2.20
Other business-persons	9.0 :	25.4 :	29.4 :	26.3 :	9.9	1.97
All	14.3 :	26.5 :	25.8 :	22.2 :	11.2	2.11

[a]0 = Strongly Disagree; 4 = Strongly Agree

Table C-13
Sex of Respondent
(Percentages)

	Male	*Female*
Security analysts	95.5	4.5
Institutional investors	98.2	1.8
Professional investors	97.0	3.0
Stockholders	93.6	6.4
Other business-persons	75.2	24.8
All	87.2	12.8

Appendix D:
Assumptions Required
for Multiple-Regression
Analysis

Significance tests associated with multiple regression are based on several assumptions:

1. The sample is drawn at random.
2. Each array of Y for a given combination of Xs follows the normal distribution.
3. The regression of Y and Xs is linear.
4. The error components
   (a) are independent;
   (b) have a mean of zero;
   (c) have the same variance throughout the range of Y values.
5. The Xs are not significantly intercorrelated.
6. All variables are interval or higher measures.

Assumption 1 is generally met with respect to the stockholders, security analysts, and institutional investors used in this experiment; their names were selected through a random-sampling process by the Dunhill list company, although the names in the full lists may not represent complete enumerations of the three populations within the United States, and, further, may not represent a random sampling from those populations. The assumption is also met for the Wichita State University students in the sense that the entire population of students in eligible classes was used. As noted in chapter 4, the characteristics of these students appear to be representative of the population of persons in business except that the group used is (1) younger than we might expect for the national population of business persons, and (2) is located in Wichita and may thus reflect a regional bias. Insofar as these persons differ from the national population in characteristics measured in this study, control was established through the multiple-regression procedure.

Assumption 2 was investigated through an examination of residuals. Except for the three attitudinal variables, these displayed positive kurtosis and thus departed from normality. However, the assumption of normal distribution may be relaxed if the sample size is large (Nie et al. 1975, p. 341). Fortunately, large samples (five groups of over 350 individuals each) were used for the five tests reported in this study. Furthermore, Cochran (1947, p. 24) suggests that "no serious error is introduced by non-normality in the significance levels of the F-test."

Nie et al. (p. 371ff) suggest a procedure for determining and achieving linearity, by adding successive powers of a predictor variable to the equation and determining whether each new polynomial term significantly increases the overall R^2. This iterative process was used to test the effect of successively higher order versions of each explanatory variable until no significant improvement in the R^2s could be obtained. Second order variables did not significantly improve the R^2s for the INVESTMENT DECISION, SHARE PRICE ESTIMATE, INCOME PROJECTION, and ASSESSMENT OF FRAUD responses. The R^2 for the CONFIDENCE RATING response was improved significantly by adding variables for EXPERIENCE, STOCK EVALUATIONS, AGE, ACTUAL DJIA, INVESTMENT DECISION, INVESTMENT ATTITUDE, and TOTAL YEARS, all raised to the second power, and for EXPERIENCE and INVESTMENT DECISION, raised to the third power. Similarly the R^2 for the COMPANY EVALUATION response was significantly improved by adding a variable for INVESTMENT ATTITUDE raised to the second power. These additions should remove all significant nonlinearity from the five estimating equations and thereby satisfy assumption 3.

Residuals were examined for assumptions 4(a), (b), and (c). All appear to be satisfied. It should be noted that time-series data are not involved in these experiments, so serial correlation is not an issue. Further, according to Cochran (1947, p. 33) the errors may be treated as if they were independent because subjects were always randomly assigned to control and test groups.

Correlation coefficients were examined to identify cases of multicollinearity. Tests were run on a number of interaction terms, constructed by multiplying the two correlated variables together, to determine which interaction terms contribute significantly to improvement in R^2. This process resulted in the addition of two interactive terms to the equation for the CONFIDENCE RATING variable, as follows:

TOTAL YEARS = Square root of EXPERIENCE times AGE

TOTAL HOURS = Square Root of ACCOUNTING HOURS times FINANCE HOURS

With these additions, assumption 5 appears to be satisfied.

Careful attention was given to the requirement of assumption 6, that all variables be interval measures. When scales were used, only the polar points were labeled. While there is still some controversy over this treatment, the consensus among social scientists is that this results in an interval measure. The only exception to the interval-measures requirement is the STOCK EVALUATIONS variable. Subjects checked one of four responses—never, rarely, occasionally, or frequently—to indicate the frequency with which they evaluate stocks or advise investors. This produces an ordinal measure. Consequently the responses on this variable were recorded as three dummy variables, one each for the last three responses. This transformation did not significantly change the multiple-regression statistics including the multiple coefficient of determination; it did, however, add two variables to the estimating equations. Since there are several advantages to minimizing the number of independent variables in an equation as long as variables that contribute significantly to the coefficient of determination are not eliminated, these additional dummy variables were eliminated in favor of treating the original stock-evaluations variable as interval.

Dummy or dichotomous variables, of course, result in an interval scale, since they assume, in this study, only the values 0 and 1.

Bibliography

AICPA. *Accounting Principles Board Statement No. 4—Basic Concepts and Accounting Principles Underlying Financial Statements of Business Enterprises*. New York: American Institute of Certified Public Accountants, 1970.

_____ . *Accounting Trends & Techniques*. 34th ed. New York: American Institute of Certified Public Accountants, 1980.

_____ . *Statement on Auditing Standards No. 1—Codification of Auditing Standards and Procedures*. New York: American Institute of Certified Public Accountants, 1972.

_____ . *Statement on Auditing Standards No. 2—Reports on Audited Financial Statements*. New York: American Institute of Certified Public Accountants, 1974.

_____ . *Statement on Auditing Standards No. 15—Reports on Comparative Financial Statements*. New York: American Institute of Certified Public Accountants, 1976.

Alderman, C. Wayne. "The Role of Uncertainty Qualifications: Evidence to Support the Tentative Conclusions of the Cohen Commission." *The Journal of Accountancy*, November 1977, pp. 97-100.

Anderson, H.M., J.W. Giese, and Jon Booker. "Some Propositions About Auditing." *The Accounting Review*, July 1970, pp. 524-531.

Arminio, Vincent P. *The Accountant's Report—Its Significance and Meaning to Credit Grantors*. Lake Success, N.Y.: Credit Research Foundation, Inc., 1970.

Armstrong, J. Scott, and Terry S. Overton. "Estimating Nonresponse Bias in Mail Surveys." *Journal of Marketing Research*, August 1977, pp. 396-402.

Arthur Andersen & Co. *Public Accounting in Transition: American Shareowners View the Role of Independent Accountants and the Corporate Reporting Controversy*. Chicago: Arthur Andersen & Co., 1974.

"ASB Opts to Keep Current Auditor's Report." *The Journal of Accountancy*, April 1981, p. 3.

Ashton, Robert H., and Sandra S. Kramer. "Students as Surrogates in Behavioral Accounting Research: Some Evidence." *Journal of Accounting Research*, Spring 1980, pp. 1-15.

Ashworth, John. "Some Further Data on the Image of the CPA—An Interim Report." *The Journal of Accountancy*, February 1963, pp. 50-55.

Bailey, William T. "An Appraisal of Research Designs Used to Investigate the Information Content of Audit Reports." *The Accounting Review*, January 1982, pp. 141-146.

Ball, Ray, R.G. Walker, and G.P. Whittred. "Audit Qualifications and Share Prices." *Abacus*, June 1979, pp. 23-34.

Barnett, Andrew Horn. "Communication in Auditing: An Examination of Investors' Understanding of the Auditor's Report." Unpublished D.B.A. dissertation, Texas Tech University, 1976.

Baskin, Elba F. "The Communicative Effectiveness of Consistency Exceptions." *The Accounting Review*, January 1972, pp. 38-51.

Beck, G.W. "The Role of the Auditor in Modern Society: An Empirical Appraisal." *Accounting and Business Research*, Spring 1973, pp. 117-122.

Benjamin, James J., and Robert H. Strawser. "The Publication of Forecasts: An Experiment." *Abacus*, December 1974, pp. 138-146.

Bennett, Jerome Vincent. "An Inquiry Into the Meanings of the Auditor's Unqualified Opinion to Stockholders, Auditors and Accountants." Unpublished Ph.D. dissertation, University of South Carolina, 1976.

Bertholdt, Richard H. "Discussion of the Impact of Uncertainty Reporting on the Loan Decision." *Journal of Accounting Research*, Supplement 1979, pp. 58-63.

Bevis, Herman W. "The CPA's Attest Function in Modern Society." *The Journal of Accountancy*, February 1962, pp. 28-35.

Brenner, Vincent C. "Are Annual Reports Being Read?—An Empirical Study." *The National Public Accountant,* November 1971, pp. 16-21.

Briloff, Abraham J. "Old Myths and New Realities in Accountancy." *The Accounting Review*, July 1966, pp 484-495.

Briston, Richard, and Robert Perks. "The External Auditor—His Role and Cost to Society." *Accountancy*, November 1977, pp. 48-51.

Burton, John C., and A. Clarence Sampson. "Future Needs for Auditing Research." *Symposium on Auditing Research*. University of Illinois at Urbana-Champaign, 1976, pp. 217-225.

Buzby, Stephen L. "Selected Items of Information and Their Disclosure in Accounting Reports." *The Accounting Review*, July 1974, pp. 423-435.

Campbell, Donald T., and Julian C. Stanley. "Experimental and Quasi-Experimental Designs for Research on Teaching." In *Handbook of Research on Teaching*, edited by N.L. Gage. Chicago: Rand McNally & Company, 1963.

Carmichael, D.R. *The Auditor's Reporting Obligation.* New York: American Institute of Certified Public Accountants, 1972.

———. "The Assurance Function—Auditing at the Crossroads." *The Journal of Accountancy*, September 1974, pp. 64-72.

Chang, Lucia S., and Kenneth S. Most. *Financial Statements and Investment Decisions.* Miami: School of Business and Organizational Sciences, Florida International University, 1979.

Clift, Robert C. "Brokers' Criticisms of Auditors." *The Chartered Accountant in Australia*, May 1973, pp. 4-8.

Cochran, W.G. "Some Consequences When the Assumptions for the Analysis of Variance Are Not Satisfied." *Biometrics*, March 1947, pp. 22-38.

Commission on Auditors' Responsibilities. *Report, Conclusions, and Recommendations*. New York: Commission on Auditors' Responsibilities, 1978.

Committee on Basic Auditing Concepts. *A Statement of Basic Auditing Concepts*. Sarasota, Florida: American Accounting Association, 1973.

Corless, John C., and Corine T. Norgaard. "User Reactions to CPA Reports on Forecasts." *The Journal of Accountancy*, August 1974, pp. 46-54.

Dillard, Jesse F., Richard J. Murdock, and John K. Shank. "CPAs' Attitudes Toward 'Subject To' Opinions." *The CPA Journal*, August 1978, pp. 43-47.

Dyckman, Thomas R., Michael Gibbins, and Robert J. Swieringa. "Experimental Survey Research in Financial Accounting: A Review and Evaluation." In *The Impact of Accounting Research on Practice and Disclosure*, edited by A. Rashad Abdel-khalik and Thomas F. Keller. Durham, N.C.: Duke University Press, 1978.

Elias, Nabil. "The Effects of Human Asset Statements on the Investment Decision: An Experiment." *Empirical Research in Accounting: Selected Studies 1972*, Supplement to *Journal of Accounting Research*, 1972, pp. 215-233.

Epstein, Marc J. *The Usefulness of Annual Reports to Corporate Shareholders*. Los Angeles: Bureau of Business and Economic Research, California State University, Los Angeles, 1975.

Estes, Ralph, and Marvin Reimer. "A Study of the Effect of Qualified Auditors' Opinions on Bankers' Lending Decisions." *Accounting and Business Research*, Autumn 1977, pp. 250-259.

_____ . "An Experimental Study of the Differential Effect of Standard and Qualified Auditors' Opinions on Investors' Price Decisions." *Accounting and Business Research*, Spring 1979, pp. 157-162.

Fess, Philip E., and Richard E. Ziegler. "Readership of the Audit Report." *The CPA Journal*, June 1977, pp. 5-6.

Firth, Michael. "Qualified Audit Reports: Their Impact on Investment Decisions." *The Accounting Review*, July 1978, pp. 642-650. Summarized in *Financial Times* (London), June 14, 1978, p. 11.

_____ . "Qualified Audit Reports and Bank Lending Decisions." *Journal of Bank Research*, Winter 1979, pp. 237-241.

Frishkoff, Paul, and Robert Rogowski. "Disclaimers of Audit Opinion." *Management Accounting*, May 1978, pp. 52-57.

Georgeson & Co. and Graham-Chisholm Company. *New Trends in Annual Report Readership: An Updated Study of Aunt Jane and the Analyst.* New York: Georgeson & Co. and Graham-Chisholm Company, 1972.

Glazer, Alan Stuart. "An Investigation of the Effects of Alternative Auditors' Reports on Investment Behavior in the Presence of Litigation Uncertainties." Unpublished Ph.D. dissertation, University of Pennsylvania, 1978.

Guy, Dan M., Roy M. Greenway, Ross M. Miller, and John C. Mills. "Audit Reports, Financial Statements and Creditor Perception." *The Texas CPA*, January 1974, pp. 5-10.

Hendricks, James A. "The Impact of Human Resource Accounting Information on Stock Investment Decisions: An Empirical Study." *The Accounting Review*, April 1976, pp. 292-305.

Horngren, Charles T. *Cost Accounting: A Managerial Emphasis.* 4th ed. Englewood Cliffs, N.J.: Prentice-Hall, Inc., 1977.

Hull, Rita P. "The Impact of Environmental Disclosure on Stock Investment Decisions: A Behavioral Experiment." Unpublished research paper, Northern Illinois University, 1980.

Kaplan, Robert S. "The Information Content of Financial Accounting Numbers: A Survey of Empirical Evidence. In *The Impact of Accounting Research on Practice and Disclosure*, edited by A. Rashad Abdel-khalik and Thomas F. Keller. Durham, N.C.: Duke University Press, 1978.

Kapnick, Harvey. "Statement Before Moss Subcommittee Hearings on the Accounting Profession and Its Self-Reform Efforts." *Arthur Andersen & Co. Executive News Briefs*, February 1978, pp. 1-6.

Knoll, M. "Auditor's Report—Society's Expectations v. Realities." *Accounting and Business Research*, Summer 1976, pp. 182-200.

Koutsoyiannis, A. *Theory of Econometrics.* New York: Barnes & Noble, 1973.

Lee, T.A. "The Nature of Auditing and Its Objectives." *Accountancy*, April 1970, pp. 292-296.

Lee, T.A., and D.P. Tweedie. "Accounting Information: An Investigation of Private Shareholder Usage." *Accounting and Business Research*, Autumn 1975a, pp. 280-291.

_____ . "Accounting Information: An Investigation of Private Shareholder Understanding." *Accounting and Business Research,* Winter 1975b., pp. 3-17.

_____ . *The Private Shareholder and the Corporate Report.* London: The Institute of Chartered Accountants in England and Wales, 1977.

Libby, Robert. "Bankers' and Auditors' Perceptions of the Message Communicated by the Audit Report." *Journal of Accounting Research*, Spring 1979a, pp. 99-122.

_____ . "The Impact of Uncertainty Reporting on the Loan Decision." *Journal of Accounting Research*, Supplement 1979b, pp. 35-57.

The New York Stock Exchange. *Shareownership 1975*. New York: The New York Stock Exchange, 1975.

Ng, David S. "Supply and Demand for Auditing Services and the Nature of Regulations in Auditing." In *"The Accounting Establishment" in Perspective: Proceedings of the Arthur Young Professors' Roundtable 1978*, edited by Sidney Davidson. Chicago: Arthur Young & Co., 1979, pp. 99-124.

Nie, Norman H., C. Hadlai Hull, Jean G. Jenkins, Karin Steinbrenner, and Dale H. Bent. *SPSS: Statistical Package for the Social Sciences*. 2nd ed. New York: McGraw-Hill Book Company, 1975.

Nunnally, Jum C. *Psychometric Theory*. 2nd ed. New York: McGraw-Hill Book Company, 1978.

Oliver, Bruce L. "The Semantic Differential: A Device for Measuring the Interprofessional Communication of Selected Accounting Concepts." *Journal of Accounting Research*, Autumn 1974, pp. 299-316.

Oppenheim, A.N. *Questionnaire Design and Attitude Measurement*. New York: Basic Books, Inc., 1966.

Peat, Marwick, Mitchell & Co. *Research Opportunities in Auditing*. New York: Peat, Marwick, Mitchell & Co., 1976.

Purdy, Charles R., Jay M. Smith, and Jack Gray. "The Visibility of the Auditor's Disclosure of Deviance from APB Opinion: An Empirical Test." *Empirical Research in Accounting: Selected Studies 1969*, Supplement to *Journal of Accounting Research*, 1969, pp. 1-18.

Reckers, Philip M.J., and Lawrence J. Gramling. "Is the 'Subject To' Audit Report Meaningful? An Experimental Investigation of Financial Analysts' Judgements." *Michigan CPA*, July-August 1979, pp. 63-68.

Sale, Dereck C. "The Auditors' Responsibilities: The Gathering Storm." *The Journal of Accountancy*, January 1981, pp. 76-86.

Schultz, Joseph J., Jr. "Discussion of the Impact of Uncertainty Reporting on the Loan Decision." *Journal of Accounting Research*, Supplement 1979, pp. 64-71.

Scott, Edward Ray. "An Empirical Test of the Stock Market Response to the Consistency Exception in Auditors' Reports." Unpublished Ph.D. dissertation, University of Illinois, 1974.

Shank, John K., Jesse F. Dillard, and Joseph H. Bylinski. "What Do 'Subject To' Auditors' Opinions Mean to Investors?" *Financial Analysts Journal*, January-February 1979, pp. 41-45.

Shank, John K., Jesse F. Dillard, and Richard J. Murdock. "How Financial Executives Regard 'Subject To' Opinions." *Financial Executive*, November 1979. pp. 28-35.

_____ . "Lending Officers' Attitudes Toward 'Subject To' Audit Opinions." *The Journal of Commercial Bank Lending*, March 1978, pp. 31-45.

Shank, John K., Richard J. Murdock, and Jesse F. Dillard. " 'Subject To' Audit Opinions: Three Capital Market Tests." Unpublished research paper, Ohio State University, December 1977.

Shannon, Claude F., and Warren Weaver. *The Mathematical Theory of Communication*. Urbana, Ill.: The University of Illinois Press, 1964.

Stobie, Bruce. "The Audit Report: A Valuable Product or a Useless Anachronism?" *The South African Chartered Accountant*, February 1978, pp. 49-57.

"What Bankers Think of CPA Services." *The Practical Accountant*, May-June 1974, pp. 52-53.

Winters, Alan J. "Banker Perceptions of Unaudited Financial Statements." *The CPA Journal*, August 1975, pp. 29-33.

Wonnacott, Ronald J., and Thomas H. Wonnacott. *Econometrics*. New York: John Wiley & Sons, 1970.

Index

About the Author

Ralph Estes is director of the School of Accountancy and professor of accounting at Wichita State University. He is the author of several books, including *Corporate Social Accounting* and *Dictionary of Accounting*, as well as over thirty scholarly articles in journals published in the United States, Canada, the United Kingdom, and Japan. He is a certified public accountant and holds a doctorate in business administration from Indiana University.